Great Things

One Girl's Path to Freedom

Tina Montoya

FINA LEGACY
—PUBLISHING—

Library of Congress Control Number: 2025936163

ISBN 979-8-9928815-0-9 (Paperback edition)
ISBN 979-8-9928815-1-6 (Ebook edition)

Marketing Manager: Victoria Hinton
Publishing Consultant: Matthew Wayne Selznick
Cover Design: Vanessa Mendozzi

Disclaimer

This memoir is a true account of my life, as I remember it. I have done my best to recount events, conversations, and emotions with honesty and integrity. Still, memory is as human as the people who hold it—shaped by time, emotion, and perspective. Some details may differ from how others remember them, but the heart of each moment remains true to my experience.

The views and opinions expressed in this memoir are mine and do not reflect those of any organizations, institutions, or individuals mentioned.

Real names of certain schools, police departments, and other institutions are used throughout this book. When they appear, they reflect my personal encounters and perceptions at the time. These depictions are not meant as sweeping judgments, but as honest portrayals of how those experiences shaped me.

Some excerpts and documents included in this memoir were obtained legally through public records requests. Identifying information has been redacted where appropriate, though certain details may remain when relevant to the story. These materials are presented as part of my personal experience and are not intended as legal claims or accusations.

Mentions of specific brands, products, or companies are used descriptively and for storytelling purposes only. All trademarks remain the property of their respective owners.

Some names and identifying details have been changed or altered to protect the privacy of individuals. Any resemblance to real people, living or dead, is purely coincidental when not explicitly acknowledged.

This is my story—imperfect, personal, and deeply true to me.

This book is dedicated to the loving memory of my mother.

Even in your short time here, the strength and courage you lived by taught me how to fight for myself—and survive.

Acknowledgments

Ava Justine dedicated countless hours—often dropping everything —during the three months leading up to publication to help me release this book on my mother's birthday. Without her, you wouldn't be reading *Great Things*.

Angela Ray breathed life into my original manuscript, and Gail Nastasia helped me work through two or three more versions. Their contributions paved the way for this book to become a reality.

For over thirty years, Karla, my counselor, helped me process my grief and become the woman I am today, and my cousin/friend, Christine, believed in me and prayed for me. I am alive today because of them both.

Many people over the years prayed for me, encouraged me, and loved me—even when I wasn't easy to love. I hope you know who you are and that you are abundantly blessed for your patience and kindness.

Contents

Chapter 1

Failure

M y hands shook, and I fidgeted uncomfortably in my desk chair as I clicked the refresh button on the Texas Board of Law Examiners' website. The words "February 2003 Bar Exam results will be available soon" appeared. The room was dark, lit only by the glow of my computer screen. I hit the refresh button again, and was met with the same message. "What the hell—why is this taking so long?" Blowing out an exasperated breath, I turned to my dogs, Bear and Amanda, for some moral support, but they were lounging in oblivion on the floor nearby, snoring in unison. I turned back to the bright screen that illuminated the room.

The results were scheduled for release on May fifth, which—coincidentally, I thought—happened to be my mother's birthday. Last year, the results were posted online between eleven-thirty and midnight the night before. Armed with that hope and three cups of strong coffee, I'd been bouncing between watching *Antwone Fisher* and hitting refresh. I was bursting at the seams. Last year's failure had been a bitter disappointment, but this time, I was sure I had passed. The signs were all there. My law school graduation had fallen on the anniversary of her death, so it only made sense I'd pass the bar on her birthday. Or at least, that was how I kept justifying it in my head, and I could almost feel my mother peering over my shoulder with each click of the mouse.

Finally, the screen changed, and I nearly jumped out of my seat. The results list appeared and, for a second, the words swirled before my eyes. I took a deep breath and began to search through the thousands of alphabetical names for mine, only to realize I was looking under my married last name—I was mid-divorce and had chosen to take my maiden name back to practice law. I was sure this must be the issue, and resumed my search under my maiden name, combing through the pages to confirm that I had passed. That last name wasn't there either. I searched again using my married name —perhaps, in my worked-up state, I had missed it?

But after painstakingly combing through the list one last time, the realization sank in. My name wasn't there.

I slumped back in my chair, feeling a sudden weight on my chest and my dinner rising in my throat. How could this be happening again? I had managed to keep my job as an associate attorney after the first failed exam, but I was certain they'd fire me this time. How would I pay my bills if my only job was delivering pizza? The thought of my hefty student loans made me suddenly nauseous.

The tears came fast as my mind raced with negative thoughts about myself. I was stupid and worthless and wouldn't amount to anything. And despite my mother's faith in me, I was not, in fact, destined for greatness. Now *everyone will know the truth—I'm a failure.*

As my thoughts spiraled, the room seemed to shrink around me and I knew I needed to escape. It was late, so going for a run was out of the question unless I wanted to end up a cautionary tale on the morning news, although maybe that would be better than facing tomorrow. And where was God right now? If He could do anything, why didn't He let me pass? Anger welled up inside me, and I went in the bathroom to splash cold water on my face. That didn't work, so I tried brushing my hair. When I was finished, I stared into the mirror at my limp, fine curls and felt even more mad. Maybe if I had a thick head of model-beautiful hair, this wouldn't matter so much?

I padded back into the bedroom in my fuzzy pink slippers— the only thing I could think of was to beat something with my tennis racket, like I'd learned in therapy.

When I finished taking my frustrations out on the bedroom pillows, I returned to my computer and shut it down, the black screen a relief. I composed myself and got to work doing what came next: calling my best friend to cancel our celebration trip to New York City. I knew she was only the first of many humiliating calls to come.

Chapter 2

Great Things

My mother was scurrying around the house in her usual navy-dress-and-pantyhose combo, trying to get out the door. She was running late on this particular Saturday morning in the early spring of 1978.

The rest of the household was fast asleep. I had been trailing behind her, begging her to take me to work with her. "I promise, Mama, I'll be good and sweep the hair. Please, Mama, please!"

I tripped over the place where the linoleum curled where it met the living room carpet, and that finally got my mother's attention. She glanced down at me and whispered. "Okay, *mija*. Wait for me at the front door. But get out of those pajamas and put on your skirt—the purple one, okay—no pants at the shop. And brush your hair."

I was bouncing off the walls with excitement. I loved being at her beauty shop, where I could tell my outlandish stories and make everyone laugh.

A few moments later, my mother slipped on her white tennis shoes and dashed out the front door, waving her hand for me to follow her. She'd recently purchased a black Chrysler New Yorker.

As I slid onto the cold red leather seat in my skirt, my legs tingled with goosebumps. I rubbed them for warmth.

The sky was gloomy, but the sun looked as though it would burst out of the clouds at any moment. I wondered what music we would be listening to on the drive. My mother enjoyed singing with Neil Diamond and Tom Jones, often snapping her fingers back and forth, quickly, to the rhythm of every song. At the stop lights, she would lower the visor and apply her makeup—sometimes a little pressed powder, or her favorite lipstick, one that didn't stray much from the natural color of her lips, which made me wonder what the point was.

Today, as she rolled the lipstick tube across her lips, I watched her profile, fascinated by the flutter of her false eyelashes.

Once we arrived at the shop, I ran straight to the cubby area, where the tiny black and white television was perched atop the towel cabinet. The television was meant to entertain the clients, who usually watched the news or soap operas while sitting under the hair dryers, so I had to change the channel. With a few scrolls of the knob, I found an episode of *Bugs Bunny*.

But I kept my promise to my mother, as always—I kept busy sweeping, folding towels, and cleaning hairbrushes in between cartoons, during the commercial breaks and when the ladies needed to be under the hair dryer, which was very loud and right by the television.

When I heard the bell that signaled the front door opening, I'd run to greet the customers. "Welcome to Jody's Beauty Shop," I told them, using my arm to guide them to the waiting area.

"Just look at your sweet little helper," one woman told my mother, patting me on the head. Most of the ladies would smile or laugh, complimenting me on how cute I was, but one of them rolled her eyes at me. I thought maybe she was having a bad day.

At noon, I took a short walk to the store a block away to buy a Coke and Cheetos—my usual routine.

As my mother locked the door behind her final customer, she

let out a sigh. Gathering the dirty towels, she tossed them into the hamper while I danced around her, filled with joy.

"Please let me wash your hair," I pleaded. "Please, Mama."

She'd usually say we didn't have time. But on that afternoon, she relented. "Okay, *mija*," she said, her laughter filling the salon.

As she sank into the worn black chair, I ran for the egg crate and slid it to the edge of the sink and jumped on top. As her gaze lifted to mine and we waited for the water to warm, I noticed her golden brown eyes were bloodshot and swollen. I smoothed her hair back and wet it, poured some shampoo into my hand, and began working it through her silky hair and massaging her scalp. I copied everything I'd seen her do, so she'd be proud.

The soap suds squished through my fingers; then I turned the water back on. "I'm going to be just like you, Mama, when I grow up," I declared.

My mother's head snapped up, causing suds to fly in all directions. I stood frozen on the crate. She slid from the chair, dropping to her knees before me. Her hands caressed my arms, their touch both comforting and intense. I met her gaze, trying to understand the mixture of emotions in her eyes.

"No," she said finally, her voice firm but soft. "You will be better than me. You're going to be a doctor or a lawyer—you're going to do great things someday."

I stared at her for a moment. She kissed my forehead and sat back in the chair for me to finish. I was typically full of questions, but this time I finished washing her hair, unsure of what had just happened.

Chapter 3

Becoming

My mother was born in El Paso, Texas, and her parents gave her a traditional Hispanic name. She was beautiful, with her jet-black mane falling to her waist and a light complexion with a golden undertone, despite her barely five-feet-tall stature. After marrying my father, she transformed her appearance, avoiding the sun and bleaching her hair blonde. She became Jody Cage. I didn't even know she was Hispanic until after she died. It was only then that I realized I had never understood her pronunciation of certain words like church or chicken, which she would say "shurch" or "shicken." It always made me laugh. In fact, I used to think she did it on purpose, until I overheard my mother's sister—who I had never met before—talking with someone else at the gravesite. It turned out that my mother's pronunciation of "chicken" was exactly like hers.

My mother's family was a mystery to me. Apart from seeing them at her funeral, my only knowledge of them came from old photographs. In one picture, my mother was wearing her *quinceañera* dress. In another, she stood between her parents, with

Ivy on her hip and Brandy standing between her legs. Looking at them, they didn't resemble me. My grandfather had a complexion as dark as a Hershey's chocolate bar, while my grandmother's skin was ivory with a golden glow. I was pale with big brown eyes, freckles, and chubby cheeks. I looked nothing like them.

Before my mother met my father, she was married to a man with a criminal record. My fifteen-year-old mother became his partner in crime. They were cat burglars in love. But after being caught and serving time in jail, she vowed to change her life. She divorced her first husband and left El Paso for Dallas, bringing my sisters, Ivy and Brandy, who were four and five years old.

I know very little about what happened during those first few months in Dallas, before my mother met my father. From hushed phone calls, spoken in a language I'd never heard she made late at night or when my father was away—I had the overall sense that my mother had secrets she wanted to leave behind. My sisters described being locked in an apartment with little food while my mother was at work. They shared stories of instances where my mother would tie them to chairs, beat them, or lock them in the closet while she entertained men.

It was difficult for me to imagine my mother in such desperate circumstances, searching for a husband. But I can understand her relief the night she met my father in a bar and realized he might be her ticket to a better life for her and her two daughters. In 1969, women and Hispanics were second-class citizens, making it almost impossible for her to survive on her own. I recall her mentioning multiple times, when she was on the phone with friends or at her shop, "I gave my girls a fighting chance by giving them a white last name."

People considered my father Caucasian, even though his complexion was dark brown. He proudly claimed to have Cherokee blood running through his veins. Of the ten children in his family, he was number nine. They called him Dub, short for Dublin. His brothers and sisters all lived together on a farm in New

Albany, Mississippi, until, one by one, they left the farm for other pursuits. His sisters always liked to say how he was great at anything he tried, any sport or hobby he picked up, and how smart he was. In elementary school, he skipped two grades, making him a prime target for bullies, and because of how difficult school became, he only made it through the sixth grade.

Although he'd been picking cotton since he was six years old, he had to get a real job at fifteen to support his mother and sister after his father's death. He moved to St. Louis, Missouri, and worked in shipyards until he turned seventeen and joined the army.

After shipping out and serving in the Korean War for two years, he came back an angry drunk. Or at least that is what I've been told.

Upon his return, my father got married, and he and wife number one had four children. The marriage ended when my father went to the restaurant where his wife worked and pointed a gun in her face. Although she managed to calm him down and no shots were fired, the police were called, and he ran. His older sister Penny, who lived in Illinois, brokered a deal with his wife—she told his wife he'd give her a divorce, leave the state, and never set foot in Illinois again if she wouldn't press criminal charges against him. My father, in exchange for his freedom, never saw his four children again.

DURING MY TODDLER PHASE, I was daddy's little girl, always seeking his approval and attention, and getting it—I was told he was just as smitten with me as I was with him. As I began to walk, my parents noticed my bowed legs. They consulted with a pediatrician, who reassured them I would outgrow it, but by two I had not.

While my mother put more faith in God, my father put more stock in medicine. She would drag me to Saint Cecilia Catholic Church, where we would light a candle, find a pew, kneel, and pray for God to heal my bowed legs. However, he would drag me to Scottish Rite Children's Hospital.

On my first visit, my medical records say I entered as a happy two-year-old, bouncing around the waiting room. At some point, once I figured out why I was there and what they were going to do to me, that must have changed—I remember my entire body shaking and feeling nauseous every time I walked through those automatic doors. Maybe it had something to do with my mom not going to these leg visits; maybe those were just too much for her. Either way, I don't remember bouncing with joy!

But there was one trip to the hospital that changed my perspective, due to my father's genius idea.

I was about four, and I remember sitting in the front seat of my father's green Dodge Demon. My legs bounced nervously as we exited the freeway. Near the barely cracked window, he held a cigarette in his left hand. As he drove, the car sucked the smoke out and cold air seeped inside. My father appeared to be deep in thought, and I tightened my grip on Winnie the Pooh.

As we turned into the parking spot, my father turned to me and said, "Baby doll, if you don't cry or fight the nurses today, I'll give you twenty dollars."

I froze. My eyes widened as I pondered his offer. Twenty dollars was a lot! "Okay," I said, sitting up perfectly straight and reaching for the door handle.

A wide grin spread across his face. "Let's see if you can do it," he said, as if he was challenging me to a duel.

We kept our routine, walking through the entrance and around the corner to the nurse's office, where blood was drawn. When our eyes met, and she realized who I was, her face fell as she grabbed the phone. "Let me call more nurses."

My father grinned. "Put her in the chair and let's see how she does."

She raised her eyebrows, and her jaw dropped. "Are you sure?"

He put the palm of his hand on my back and guided me to the red school desk where kids would sit for their blood draws.

I took off my coat, squeezed Winnie the Pooh with my left hand, and put my right arm on the desk. "I'm four now. And a big girl," I said with a trembling voice. I wanted her to know my father wasn't kidding, that we really didn't need those other nurses.

My father nodded to the nurse, signaling that she go ahead.

My whole body tightened as I held my breath and felt the needle's prick. A single tear escaped from my eye. "Are you crying?" my father demanded.

I yelled back, "No, I'm not!"

The nurse turned to him as she finished up. "What did you do?" she asked, looking at him in wonder.

"I offered her money," he said with a giggle. She shook her head, crossed her arms, and leaned against the door as we walked out of her office. He responded with, "Anyone can be bought."

"Such a shame you didn't think of that two years ago," she said, raising an eyebrow and smiling.

THE CAUSE of my bowed legs perplexed the doctors. They could not confirm a diagnosis. Despite knowing I'd receive twenty dollars per trip, I dreaded the thirty-minute drive to Scottish Rite. The visits were not fun, especially the one where I left with a contraption that caused me more agony than I ever imagined my bowed legs could cause. At the visits after that, they would adjust the braces each time. It was pure torture. I think I must have blocked some of it, because my sisters later shared with me how one of them had to hold me as the other strapped me into a mermaid splint.

I have no memory of them pinning me down, and I don't remember feeling any pain from the splint itself, but I'll never forget the pain I felt when wearing braces on my feet. I had progressed to a device featuring a bottom metal bar, securing the shoes at its opposite ends. The new contraption provided constant pressure to my legs that forced my bones into proper alignment. Lying on my back all night long with my feet pointed toward the ceiling was uncomfortable, but the ache in my bones from my legs being twisted in the opposite direction was excruciating. My sisters told me I cried myself to sleep countless times. I have a few vivid memories of sobbing at night, pleading with someone to take the braces off my feet.

Over time, my bones became stronger and straighter, much to the surprise of the doctors. They thought I might need surgery and wanted a sample of my bone marrow, for research, but my mother refused—she was certain that God had healed my legs and didn't want to expose me to any more suffering.

Soon after my eighth birthday, the doctor made a note in my medical records: "The only question regarding our previous diagnosis of metaphyseal dysostosis is the x-rays done a year ago were entirely normal and the changes noted previously have disappeared, and they shouldn't have." This was my mother's proof that God had healed me—the irregularities in my x-rays had mysteriously and miraculously vanished.

MY FATHER's flexible schedule made it easy for him to take me to my appointments—he was working in West Dallas at my uncle's convenience store, Miller's Drive-In. They made hot meals and stocked snacks, groceries, and anything else you might need in a pinch. The business was a staple in the center of a violent, impoverished neighborhood where crime was rampant, and gunshots could be heard at any time of the day. Which is why my father never left home without a gun.

He always carried a revolver on his hip when he was working. Not that it deterred the robbers. Police arrested him once for aggravated assault with a deadly weapon. He had pointed a gun at a female patron and ordered her to leave when she accused him of shortchanging her. My father had a thing about pointing guns at women, it seemed. The officer's report stated, "Suspect was drunk and offense plead to disorderly conduct, time served one day."

My father also bragged about chasing a robber down the street and shooting him in the back. No arrest or investigation appeared on his record, and I had a good idea why.

After one of my trips to Scottish Rite, I had begged to go back to work with my father. I wanted to spend some of my twenty dollars on junk food.

I was busy playing with my Barbies on the floor, and with my back turned to the counter, I barely noticed when two police officers walked in to say hello. I didn't pay them much attention since I knew cops stopped by often as part of their routine patrol. I kept playing as my father greeted them.

"Howdy, officers," he said.

"Hey, Dub," the older one replied. "Looks like you don't have a thing to worry about anymore—we took care of it and planted a gun on that nigger."

In an instant, my head snapped around as I inhaled quickly. The youngest officer's face drained of color when his eyes met mine. He seemed shocked and immediately turned his gaze toward my father.

"I didn't know anyone was here with you," he stammered.

Their attention shifted to me, and a strange feeling crept into my stomach. My father made light of their concern, waving a dismissive hand in my direction, saying, "She's five—way too young to understand what's going on."

While my father and the older officer resumed their conversation, the young officer's eyes remained fixed on me. My heart was banging like a drum, even though I wasn't sure why. What I did know was that I'd heard something I shouldn't have, and that it would be good if I pretended to be a silly, dumb kid who didn't understand grownup stuff. I glanced down at the brown paper bags under the counter. "That's what I need!" I shouted, grabbing one from under the counter. I turned back to my toys and fumbled with the bag, not knowing what to do with it.

"She's just playing. See?" my father whispered. Then they teased the rookie for fearing what a little girl might have overheard.

Driving back home with my father that evening, I knew better than to ask questions, and kept my thoughts to myself.

Chapter 4

Dilly Bars

I stood at the base of the cement stairs, taking it all in before rushing up to the porch of our new home in Oak Cliff. Finally, we could move in. While my parents waited to close on the triplex, we'd been squatting in a roach-infested condemned building where the cockroaches would scatter for cover when the lights turned on at night. I'd run from them, screaming and crying. My mother would stuff cotton in my ears before I went to bed each night to keep the bugs from crawling inside.

But now, we could leave the roaches behind. I climbed the cement steps and took it all in.

We would live in the main portion of the red brick house, snuggled between two small apartments that my parents could rent out. They had already rented the efficiency apartment to Uncle Jack. He had a daughter that would be coming to visit on the weekends, and she was same age as me. Everything was looking up!

I twirled around on the porch before peering through the large window. When I yanked open the screen door, what I saw inside made me gasp; the living room was enormous. I glanced at my father standing beside me and raced through the heavy oak door.

"We have a television!" I said as I climbed onto the couch, and then immediately jumped off to run around the coffee table while keeping my eyes on the magic box.

He ruffled my hair. "Be careful around that table. It's harder than your head."

"Okay, Daddy."

Upon hearing the sounds of my family walking through the rest of the house, I diverted my attention from the living room and moved toward my mother's voice. Moving quickly, I ran right into the back of her. She smiled at me. We were all thrilled with our new home.

Down the hall, I could hear my older sisters, Brandy and Ivy, arguing. Curious, I followed their voices to the bedroom we would be sharing. They were bickering about the amount of space they would each have, but that didn't matter to me. I was just happy to be sharing a room with them. I stood there watching them argue, neither of them noticing me in the doorframe—Brandy had a scowl on her pretty face and Ivy, with her athletic calves, looked poised to pounce. They were perfect older sisters—for all I cared, they could put my bed in the closet.

OUR FAMILY QUICKLY FOUND A ROUTINE. In the mornings, once we'd had breakfast together, we would go our separate ways.

Ivy and I would walk to the elementary school a few blocks away from the house. She was in sixth grade, while I was starting kindergarten. In the afternoons, once we got home, Ivy would call our mom at work to let her know we had arrived safely—this was an established rule. Our parents had warned us not to talk to strangers, and that they could be dangerous. If we were ever more than a few minutes late returning from school, we knew we would have to visit the switch tree with our father that evening.

ONE WARM SPRING DAY, I discovered why my parents were so afraid. It happened as we were walking our regular route home from school, and as usual, we passed by the photography shop. Whenever we caught sight of the tall, round man peering at us through the blinds of his store, we'd walk faster. But this time, something unexpected occurred—he opened the door and leaned against the frame with a grin on his face. The sight of him sent a chill down my spine.

"Hey there, little girls. You want some candy?"

I sensed danger and edged away, but Ivy proceeded to move toward him.

"No!" I yanked her arm, trying to protect her.

"What are you afraid of, little girls? I'm not going to hurt you."

Ivy must have woke up and felt the danger too, because suddenly her expression changed. Her mouth hung open and her eyes widened as she turned to grab my hand. Without hesitation, we sprinted the rest of the way home, convinced we had just narrowly escaped death.

That evening, Ivy told our parents, and they immediately called the police. We never walked to school again and later learned that the man was arrested for luring children into his studio and subjecting them to unspeakable acts. Even after he was arrested and taken away, my parents continued to drive us to school every single day.

I cannot say for sure if the story was true or if they fabricated it to put the fear of God in us, but regardless, it worked.

For a little while, anyway.

ON A HOT AND HUMID AFTERNOON, my mother took us home after school. After bringing us inside, she walked the two blocks back to her beauty shop. We had a window air conditioner unit in the living room, but we weren't allowed to use it until evening time.

Just as she had left, Ivy turned to me and exclaimed, "I know a great way for us to cool off. Let's go to Dairy Queen and get a Dilly Bar."

I hesitated and said, "But Mama works right across the street."

"Scared?" she asked, poking me in the stomach.

Truth be told, I was terrified, but my desire for ice cream outweighed my fear, so I mustered up the courage to join her. With determination, I jumped to my feet and pushed the front door open.

As we made our way around the back of the house toward Dairy Queen, I paused for a moment. Out of the corner of my eye, I noticed the switch tree. I turned my attention to the long, wispy branches, remembering the last time I had to decide which one to cut for my father to whip me with. I didn't want to think about that.

Neither of us spoke a word as we walked side by side. Nearing the six-lane road and my mother's salon, I begged Ivy to tell me her plan. In response, she simply laughed.

"You see that field right there? Across from Mama's shop?"

"Yeah," I said, nodding.

She leaned in and whispered, "I'm going to creep through the grass, and you'll run toward the corner of her shop. While you watch her through the window, I'll get our ice cream and, on your signal, I run over to you and we sprint back home."

I trembled as I followed Ivy's instructions and hurried along the sidewalk to the salon. Taking a deep breath, I peered around the edge of the building and into the glass, afraid of being caught and unable to yell anything to Ivy in order to communicate with her. Instead, I waved my arm frantically and mouthed, "Go now." Ivy darted across the street. I thought of when I'd watched some kids playing dodgeball. Ivy looked very much like she was playing dodgeball, but with cars instead of the inflated ball.

That made it feel more like fun, and I suddenly felt braver.

She made it across the street and disappeared inside. As I anxiously waited for her, my head swiveling back and forth between Mama and Dairy Queen, until Ivy finally came out. I sighed in relief and raised my hand to signal her to wait a second. Glancing into the window to make sure we had the all clear, I motioned for Ivy to come as soon as my mother was distracted.

With her again by my side, we ran all the way home, where we sat on the porch enjoying our half-melted ice cream.

LIFE AT HOME SEEMED GOOD—UNTIL my father started sneaking away on what my mother would call "one of his alcohol binges." On those days, my mother would call to warn us he was drunk and on his way home to us. As soon as the call ended, my sisters and I would scramble to gather whatever we needed to hold us over for a few hours. We'd hide in one of the small outbuildings in the backyard to avoid him altogether until my mother came home from work. Two very opposite personality scenarios existed when he drank—it was either lovey-dovey Dub or mean Dub, and you never knew which one would show up.

We weren't willing to risk it.

Once inside, we'd huddle together, trying to stay warm or cool, depending on the time of year, and wait for my mother. Once my father passed out for the evening, she'd come get us and usher us back inside.

There was one time, though, when I didn't make it out of the house quickly enough.

"Oh, crap!" I heard Brandy shout as she slammed the phone down. "Mama called—Daddy's on his way home and he's drunk."

We had no clue how long we had before he would burst through the door.

I dropped my baby dolls on the floor and followed behind my

sisters, who were gathering food in the kitchen. It was at that moment when my father's car pulled up out front. Now the only escape route was to jump out of the side door in the kitchen, which didn't have any outside stairs. The drop to the ground was almost as tall as me. Brandy and Ivy jumped first and took off running. I stood on the threshold, willing my five-year-old legs to move. But I could only hear the doctor's voices in my head saying, "She can't run and jump like other kids—her bones are too fragile and they might break."

A moment later, Ivy came back for me. "Jump. Just jump!"

When the screen door creaked, I started to cry. I was terrified of jumping and terrified of staying.

We both heard the keys rattling in the front door. "Go hide," Ivy whispered urgently. "Go hide in their room!"

My room was by the front door, so Ivy's idea was a good one—I'd never make it to my room in time. I raced through the kitchen to my parents' bedroom, searching for a hiding spot. I bent down and saw that junk cluttered the space under their bed, removing that was not an option, so I had no choice but to squeeze behind their bedroom door, next to my father's shotgun.

The anticipation was unbearable as I listened to my father crash around the house before stumbling into the kitchen and opening the refrigerator. It sounded like he was making a cheese and mayonnaise sandwich—he made that one a lot. I waited quietly. Finally, he came into the bedroom, and I peeked around the door to see him fall onto the mattress. I was praying he wouldn't spot me, and that he would fall quickly into a deep sleep, so I could escape.

My heart raced as I fidgeted, struggling to stay in that cramped space and keep my body flat against the wall. But a few minutes later, I heard his loud snore. Still, I didn't move, waiting a little longer to be certain. Once I was sure he was sound asleep, I crept out of the room, tiptoed to the front door, and stepped outside into the chilly night to find my sisters.

Before long, I taught myself how to jump out the kitchen door, so I would have that as an option.

With our father's unpredictable nature in mind, we were careful to stick to this after-school routine of escaping to the outbuilding. It often felt like forever that we were in there. But once it was safe, my mother would come for us and put us to bed. Sometimes it was an hour, and sometimes it was two or three.

Chapter 5

Sticks and Stones

The racial tension at my school was at a boiling point in 1977. Just before I entered the first grade, the Dallas Independent School District had finally begun its major desegregation initiative. Over twenty years earlier, a federal judge had ordered the desegregation, but the mandate had been ignored. This did not sit well with my father, who was unhappy about the bussing of students.

A few months into the new school year, Ivy was sent home for fighting because she called someone a racist name. It seemed that Ivy had adopted my father's beliefs about people with dark skin, which made no sense to me. I had a few classmates that had darker skin, and they didn't seem any different than me. The heaviness of the day was weighing in the air as we took our seats for dinner that night. To my huge surprise, my father praised Ivy, telling her, "Good job standing up for what's right—those niggers and wetbacks don't belong at your school."

The bite I'd taken of my pork chop nearly fell out of my mouth, and it suddenly occurred to me where Ivy may have been picking up the racist names.

During his rant about second-class citizens, my mother kept

her head down and her mouth shut. For obvious reasons, she didn't feel the same way as he did—she had always taught me that everyone was equal, no matter how different they might seem from us.

THE NEXT DAY, the principal requested a meeting with my father. I'd only been in school maybe two hours when a lady from the office came to get me out of class. Ivy was with her. I heard my father's voice down the hallway as we walked to the school office, and someone else's voice, telling him if he didn't leave they'd call the police.

"You do that!" my father yelled. "I'll kill you and everyone in here if you do!"

He drilled Ivy on the way home. "Who threw the first punch?" he asked. "And did you finish it?" he asked, when she had denied starting the fight. "You better have won, because no one in this family gets their ass beat by anyone."

Later that night, my mother told us that we would be transferring to a new school. Ivy's fighting had gotten out of hand and one teacher had gotten physical with her—we were out of options. We stayed out of school for a few days and then started at Tyler Street Christian Academy.

I enjoyed Tyler Street, but I despised wearing the uniform—especially the stiff dresses. But it was structured and orderly, unlike my home life and the other schools I had attended, and I welcomed that change. At Tyler Street, the classes were smaller, and the teachers seemed more prepared and organized. It seemed like they actually cared about whether I was learning something or not. Maybe it was because they weren't dealing with discipline problems that came along with kids from the wrong side of the tracks—there were no poor kids at Tyler Street. Maybe it was because the private-school kids were better educated to begin with. Either way, being at Tyler Street gave me peace.

I was a good student and hard worker, and always finished my school assignments quickly, which left me staring at the big black-and-white clock, waiting for recess. My teacher attempted to keep me busy by helping her with projects, but that only worked for a little while before I became bored with the busy work of cutting things out, sharpening pencils, or organizing things in the teacher's supply cabinet. It was close to the end of first grade, and I had a great idea. *If I help my classmates with their schoolwork, we'll get to recess quicker.* So that's what I did. My plan did not go over well with my teacher, and I got into a little trouble. But it was good fun while it lasted! It made me feel important, helping my friends out.

I would start with giving the answers to the student to my left and right and then try to convince them to pass the answers down. Then I would run to the end of the table, close to the classroom door, when the teacher was busy looking in her supply cabinet. Since her desk was on the complete other side of the room, it was easier to hide. However, someone usually told on me before I even made it to the end of the table. The first two times she caught me, I had to stand in the corner. On the third time, I was sent to the principal's office.

I enjoyed recess more than anything. I would create all sorts of competition games for us to play. I would walk on the playground and say, "Okay, who wants to see who can make it all the way across the monkey bars the fastest?" The girls would roll their eyes and say, "You are such a tomboy—have fun playing with your boyfriends."

And I did.

I finished first grade without any big problems other than hitting a boy on the playground who had kissed me on the cheek.

I ALMOST MADE it through the entire year of second grade at Tyler Street, but I had begun interrupting the class too much, and my teacher wanted me out of her classroom. One afternoon, my father showed up to school early. I found out the principal had called him for a meeting. I was pulled out of class to join him.

"We need to pass Tina up to fourth grade next year, instead of third," the principal said. "She's been too disruptive in class, and we think it's because she's bored."

I was excited by what he was saying—I would get to be with the bigger kids! And skip a whole year of boring school! My father simply said, "Thank you" and nothing else. He shook the principal's hand and we left. I had never considered myself to be smart, but my Aunt Colette had always said my father was a genius. Maybe I could be as smart as him. Although she also said he didn't have sense enough to come in out of the rain, whatever that meant.

I couldn't wait to tell Mama the good news.

THAT NIGHT AT DINNER, I spilled the beans. "Mama, the principal said I'm going to skip third grade and go straight to fourth!"

My father stayed quiet. A little while later, while my mother cleaned up the table, she asked my father what he thought about me skipping a grade.

"I don't think it's a good idea."

Panic started to creep in. Did he think I wasn't smart enough? I really wanted to be smart, and skipping a grade would mean that for sure.

"But I've worked so hard," I pleaded. "I sit in the corner every night after dinner, memorizing my addition, subtraction, and multiplication tables."

My father wasn't listening.

"I skipped two grades in school, and I was picked on," he finally said. "I'm not letting that happen to you."

"But, Daddy, I'm big for my age, and it's only one grade."

He wouldn't budge. "You'll be starting a new school in the fall

25

and you'll be going into the third grade," he said, snapping and pointing his finger toward my bedroom.

That night, I cried myself to sleep.

I STARTED third grade at Beverly Hills Baptist School. By the time my mother finished the enrollment process on the first day of school, classes had already begun for the day. My sisters went to their classrooms, and a lady in the office walked me to mine. The third grade teacher walked over to us and grabbed my hand and led me to the front of the classroom and said, "Everyone, this is Tina."

I smiled, waiting for a group hello, but instead, a boy yelled out from the middle of the room: "Teener Wiener!" The whole class laughed. I could feel my face turning red. Despite the urge to cry, I refused to show them any sign of weakness.

A few boys singled me out over the next few days, hurling hurtful names and mocking my hair and secondhand clothing. I didn't dare tell my father because I knew he would order me to teach them a lesson on the playground, and I wasn't quite ready for that.

I ignored them mostly, but it was becoming more difficult as the year went by. When I finally told my mother what was happening, she said, "The next time, you tell them, sticks and stones may break my bones, but your words can never hurt me." Her advice, which I took the very next day, only made things worse. They started mocking me even more.

I decided a good old-fashioned challenge might do the trick. At lunch time, I walked outside to where the boys were playing soccer and, with my new best friend standing next to me, said, "We want to play."

All ten of them exploded in laughter. "Girls can't play soccer," one spouted.

"Yes, we sure can, and better than you. I think you're all a bunch of scaredy cats," I said with my right hand on my hip.

26

"Fine, let's let them play and show them they don't belong here," the ringleader said.

I nodded, and we started to play. As I rushed the kid who had the ball, stealing it from him and passing to my teammate, everything changed, and suddenly we were all equals and having the times of our lives. And we were absolutely better than the boys, so much so that, from that day forward, my best friend and I had to play against each other and were assigned to opposite teams. That was when I decided sports were going to be a lifesaver for me.

It made sense. Being active in sports seemed to be bringing my sisters immense satisfaction—and attention—in any case. Ivy played basketball and softball, and Brandy played volleyball and was a cheerleader. My father was always beaming when watching Ivy play basketball—he seemed to love that sport more than softball. I wanted to be just like my sisters and I'd decided I would play basketball and also be a cheerleader when I grew up.

Ivy and my father would practice basketball in the backyard. He wanted her to have the best layup on the team. I'd have to wait forever before we could play horse. While I was waiting, I would sit under a tree and drift off into a daydream. It would always start the same way—I'd be dribbling the ball down the court, jumping to land the perfect layup that would win us the game. The crowd would erupt, and I'd turn to see my whole family on their feet cheering me on. Of course, I couldn't celebrate long, because I'd have to quickly change into my cheerleading outfit and run out onto the court to cheer for the boys. My family would yell and cheer while I performed my cheerleading duties to the utmost perfection. Then my father would pick me up and say, "We'll play horse next time—it's time for dinner."

It was always a good daydream.

And other than getting picked on by the girls for being a tomboy, which didn't bother me one bit, the rest of the school year was a breeze.

SUMMER WAS FINALLY HERE and brought rollercoaster rides at Six Flags and my belly full of hot dogs and cherry slushes. On some Friday nights, my father would take us roller-skating, where I'd be hopped up on coke and candy, circling the rink and waving at him as I passed by. My best friend would meet us there, and we would skate until our legs wobbled with exhaustion.

But what I enjoyed most were the long Sundays at my Aunt Colette and Uncle Chester's house. We'd all pile into my mother's white Marquis and drive thirty minutes east. As we walked up the driveway, I could hear honky-tonk music playing on the stereo from the backyard and the sounds of people splashing in the pool. Opening the black iron gate, we'd be greeted with somebody yelling, "Dub and Jody are here!" I would look over and see my relatives playing poker around the small round glass top on the patio, or two-stepping to Hank Williams Jr.'s "Family Tradition."

Proceeding to the game room, I could expect to hear things like "eight ball, corner pocket" followed by the loud crack of a cue ball. Excitedly, I would ask, "Can I play? Can I play?" while jumping up and down. I was too short for the nine-foot pool table, and I had to use the bridge stick, and the adults would entertain me for a while before I tired of losing and went for a swim. They never took it easy on me, and I loved that.

As evening approached, Uncle Chester would head outside to throw some steaks, baked potatoes, and ears of corn on the grill.

After dinner, we'd usually head home, but if my mother didn't join us that day, we would hang around until late in the evening. With my belly stuffed, I'd wander into the smoke-filled game room, where the poker game had been moved. By that time, my father and the other adults were all drunk. Excited to learn more, I'd trot over.

"What are y'all playing?"

"Seven-Card Stud."

I knew if I wanted to stay, it would be smart to keep quiet. I would circle the table, carefully studying every player's hand, and observing their strategies. One night, when I was eight years old, they didn't have enough players to have a big pot. I had been waiting for my moment and begged them to let me play. Following a long lecture on losing money, my father spotted me five bucks and I played my first poker game and fell in love. My mother would have been horrified if she had known of my newfound interest in gambling. I somehow knew that and didn't mention it to her.

By the end of the summer, I had become a card shark, like my father. And while he hated losing to me, he always had a certain smile on his face that I'd not seen until we started playing poker together. While looking down and counting his money, he'd say, "If I'm going to lose, I'd rather it be to my flesh and blood than to you losers."

Everyone would laugh, but I was still and quiet in my chair, glowing inside. Finally, I'd made my father proud.

Chapter 6

AB Negative

I vy and I were enjoying summer and staying cool from the Texas heat. We had a box fan in our bedroom window, next to the bed, so we'd stripped down into shorts and tank tops and were laying on the bed listening to music. Our peaceful day took a sudden turn as my mother burst into the house. "Get in the car!" she yelled urgently. "Your father and Brandy were in an accident. We have to go to the hospital."

Ivy and I exchanged a glance, but neither of us said anything. We followed her. Since she was the oldest, Ivy rode in the front.

The minute my mother punched the gas pedal, the force sent me sliding across the scorching red leather seat, crashing into the door. The speed of her New Yorker tossed my seven-year-old body around as if I were a rag doll. I held onto the door handle as we raced toward the hospital.

I had so many questions going through my head, yet I didn't dare ask. My mother's calm eyes had a look of fear in them. They met mine in the rearview mirror, and as I began to say something, her eyes darted to the road, and I thought it best to stay quiet.

I became more and more anxious as we neared Parkland. *Was Brandy going to be okay? What about daddy?*

The tires squealed as my mother pulled into a parking spot, slamming the shifter into park. The New Yorker rocked as we jumped out. She rushed toward the front entrance with Ivy close behind her. I moved as quickly as my legs would allow. Hesitating before reaching the automatic sliding doors, I had no choice but to race through them, since they didn't slow down to wait for me. The second I was inside, memories of previous visits to Scottish Rite spun in my head. In my mind, nothing good happened at hospitals. Each time I stepped through the hospital doors, dizziness and nausea overwhelmed me. And this time was no different. In fact, it was worse, because I was scared someone might be dead. As soon as I thought it, I quickly stuffed the thought away.

The sounds of machines beeping and people talking flooded my senses as we approached the help desk and my mother told them who we were. Then my mother disappeared through the doors labeled ICU before I could ask where she was going. Ivy grabbed my arm and led me to a row of white plastic chairs in the waiting area.

"You're too young to go in there," she said, pointing at one of the chairs. I sat as directed and she sat down next to me.

We waited in silence, an hour or more passing before the doors swung open with a loud whoosh. My mother walked over to us, sliding into the chair beside Ivy. Her body slumped forward, her hands on her head.

"Horrible accident," she finally said. "Brandy died."

The news hit me as if I had been punched in the stomach. Brandy was dead? I held my breath. *She's going to be okay*, I told myself. *Wile E. Coyote never dies.* Everything felt like it had stopped. On the edge of my seat, I turned to face my mother, and Ivy did the same.

She faced us, saying, "But they brought her back."

My body relaxed as I sighed and leaned into my chair. I was right.

"Brandy and your father both have major head injuries," she explained as tears slipped from her eyes. "She's still in surgery—they don't know if she'll make it."

The surrounding noises were muffled, as if I were underwater.

"We can go inside and see your father now," she said, standing up.

Ivy and I followed her through the double doors and along the brightly lit hallway. Passing several individual rooms, we eventually stopped in front of one of them, and my mother turned to face us.

"Whatever you do, don't upset your father," she whispered. "You need to be strong."

She opened the door, allowing me to rush inside while Ivy lagged behind. As I approached the man lying down in the narrow bed, I could see that he didn't quite resemble my father. His face was puffy and bruised, and he had a cut that went from the bridge of his nose to his hairline that had been stitched up with black thread. But his eyes looked like his when they turned to me.

"Daddy, you look like Frankenstein."

He smiled and laughed. "Are you glad to see me?" he asked, his voice dry and raspy.

I moved closer and swung my leg up onto the bed, reaching my arm up in an attempt to touch the huge gash that ran from the bridge of his nose to his hairline. But my mother intervened, slipping her arms under mine and lifting me off.

That was when I noticed his right leg was suspended in the air from a trapeze-like contraption. I giggled to myself, thinking, *I guess Frankenstein is an acrobat.*

"Did Colette answer?" my father asked.

My mother nodded. "Yes. They're on their way to get the girls."

Before we had to leave, he leaned over to give me a quick hug. I couldn't quite wrap my arms around him, and there were tubes and wires in the way. There were things I wanted to know, like whether he would be able to walk, and if Brandy would live, but my mother had told me to be strong. So that's what I did—I pretended everything was just fine.

As we rode to Aunt Colette and Uncle Chester's house, with my uncle at the wheel and my aunt in the passenger seat, neither of them saying much. Ivy, sitting behind my uncle, had drifted off to sleep. I sat behind my aunt, gazing out the window at the bright full moon.

To pass the time, I played my usual game—trying to guess the next exit sign. Since Ivy was asleep, I whispered the names in my head, testing my memory: *Beckley . . . Marsalis . . . Ewing . . . Colorado.* I had invented the game to keep from being bored, a quiet challenge against myself. After a few minutes, my mind began to wander.

I started thinking back to how happy I was when I stayed with Aunt Colette and Uncle Chester before I started kindergarten. Her children were in high school when I was born, and she had volunteered to care for me, since both of my parents worked full time.

As we passed the last highway exit, I closed my eyes and remembered the nice feeling—I had felt both safe and loved when I stayed with them. In the mornings, Uncle Chester would have gone off to work by the time my aunt and I woke up. Aunt Colette would make me anything I wanted for breakfast: eggs, homemade biscuits and gravy, oatmeal, or cereal. My wish was her command. We'd spend the day cleaning the house together, which I loved because I just wanted to be near her. Throughout the day, she would surprise me and grab me and kiss me two or three times, telling me how much she loved me. After we would finish cleaning, we'd ride around in her white Cadillac, running errands, shopping, or visiting her friends.

I felt the car lurch, and it snapped me out of my fairytale world. We had arrived at Aunt Colette's house.

Ivy and I went to the bedroom where we stayed during sleepovers. Other family members had gathered in the kitchen, wanting updates. Our bedroom door was slightly ajar, and as I crawled into the bed, I could hear them just outside, talking about Brandy's condition.

"Brandy was thrown through the windshield," a woman was saying. "Parkland can't perform her next surgery until they receive more blood donations. Brandy has a rare type, AB negative."

"Do we know anyone that can donate?" a man added.

My thoughts wandered to the fight I had with Brandy the day before. I had wanted to be pretty like her, and I was playing dress-up with her clothes. I had put on her favorite pair of high heels with the clear plastic straps, her silver charm necklace, a few bracelets, a black headband with red flowers, and was carrying her black cloth purse on my shoulder.

I was staring at her makeup, thinking maybe I should do that too, when she saw me. She ran at me, screaming, "You little bitch, I told you not to touch my stuff. Take that shit off." After quickly taking all of Brandy's stuff off, with her yelling at me the whole time, I ran to my parent's bedroom crying, where I explained to my father what had happened, and told him the bad word my sister had called me. He stormed out of the room.

Wide-eyed, I turned to my mother, who tilted her head to the side and frowned. I knew what that meant; I shouldn't have tattled on Brandy.

"Don't you ever call your sister a little bitch, you hear me?" he yelled, right before I heard the smack that followed.

Brandy wouldn't even look at me when I went to bed that night.

Ivy's nudging pulled me back into the moment. She was already under the covers and trying to sleep. "Tina," she said, "get up and turn off the light. What's wrong with you?"

I didn't answer—I just got up and turned the light off, obeying her instructions.

I peeked through the slightly open door, looking around at the grownups standing in Aunt Colette's living room wondering what they would think of me if they knew how horrible I had been to Brandy right before the car accident. If Brandy died, I thought, that would be my last memory of us together.

EARLY THE NEXT MORNING, Ivy and I were eating breakfast at Uncle Chester's convenience store, when one of the regular customers walked in.

"Tyrone," Uncle Chester said, "go across the street and tell everybody that Dub's daughter needs blood, and if they go to Parkland today and donate, we'll pay them twenty dollars each."

"Yessir, Mr. Chester," Tyrone said as he turned to run out of the store.

"Tell them to bring me the receipt from Parkland, and I'll get them paid!" Uncle Chester yelled before the door swung shut. Then he looked over at Aunt Colette and said, "That Dub sure can think, even when he's laid up."

It reminded me of the time my father and I were at Scottish Rite and he told the nurse, "Anyone can be bought," right after he'd bribed me to be good with twenty dollars.

And he was right about that, because Brandy got her surgery.

Upon being released from the hospital, my father was advised to rest. The doctors said it would take at least six weeks for his broken leg to heal, and they recommended he stay off it. But that meant he couldn't work. As a garment cutter, he had to walk back and forth constantly, spreading fabric on a twenty-four-foot table. Since bills were piling up, and the woman who jumped the median with her Trans Am and hit my father's van didn't have insurance, we were in what my father called "financial trouble." I was old enough to understand that meant we were running low on cash.

While my mother worked during the day and spent her nights at the hospital with Brandy, I did my best to help by staying out of the way and taking care of myself. Each morning, I got up early, got dressed, and had breakfast on my own.

After my father had been on the couch for a whole week, he realized he couldn't afford to take any more time off. He took me to work with him. Brandy had always been the one to assist him, and now, not only was she gone, but he was far from his best.

He slowly maneuvered himself behind the wheel of the Dodge Demon, lifting his broken right leg up and laying it across the passenger floorboard. Driving with his left foot, we made our way to the shop. Upon arrival, he climbed out of the car, inched up the steps on crutches, opened the door, and got to work.

He hobbled up and down spreading fabric for hours. I did my best to keep it flat and unwrinkled on my side, but that was difficult, since the table was high up and I was only eye level with it. After my father secured the patterns with pins on top of the stack of material, he started cutting, I waited for him to push the bundles to me. Perched atop of the table, I eagerly anticipated them sliding to me.

I stood up, wrapped a thin strip of fabric around the bundle, and pulled as hard as I could, tying it like a shoelace. I used all the strength in my whole body to securely tie the string. My father had to come behind me to tighten the bigger stacks, but I made it a bit faster for him—or at least I think I did.

I went with him every day. But despite my help, he couldn't keep up his previous productivity and he lost contracts one by one —that was how he explained it to my mom, anyway. It was more of that thing he had called "financial trouble," that much I knew. I just wasn't a big enough help. The bills continued to pile up.

Brandy survived her surgery and remained in the hospital for several weeks before being transferred to a rehab facility, where she stayed for a few weeks. I was excited for her to come home, but that wasn't what ended up happening. Instead, my parents took her to my cousin's house. Tara and Brandy were close, so it kind of made sense—they both had a feisty side to them, and Brandy once said

Tara was the kind of person you would want in a dark alley with you, but I also saw that she had a sweet, caring side. She was a little older than Brandy—twenty-three—and she could have been a model with her long black hair and sky-blue eyes. She'd been living with her boyfriend, and since she wasn't working, she was available to care for Brandy.

Because Brandy had suffered a pretty bad head injury, she had to relearn all the basics: walking, talking, eating, and all sorts of other things too. She couldn't brush her teeth or tie her shoes. She was like a hundred-pound baby who couldn't do anything for herself, and it wasn't long before Tara grew frustrated with her.

A couple of weeks after Brandy had been released from rehab to live with our cousin, Tara showed up at our home with her.

"Listen," she said. "Brandy is pissing and shitting all over my house. I didn't sign up for this." She looked upset, and I guessed that she didn't feel good about having to call it quits.

But this was good news for me—I jumped up, excited to see my sister. Brandy was standing behind Tara, near the door, staring at the floor. When I ran to hug her, she looked up, pushed me to the side, and waddled over to the sofa. It was like she didn't know me at all. And if she did, she sure hadn't missed me. *What was wrong with her?* I hurried to my room and cried.

WE WERE STILL on summer break, and my parents needed somebody to watch Brandy while they worked. She couldn't do much for herself, and behaved as if she were a toddler. They couldn't afford a private sitter service so they left her with Ivy and me. I thought if I could take care of Brandy, maybe things would be better.

I'd help her get ready in the morning, brushing her teeth and her hair. I'd remind her to go potty when I did. Ivy would make sure we had lunch—it was usually hot dogs or bologna sandwiches and chips. Brandy loved grape soda, so we'd give her that. It was one of the few things that made her happy.

Brandy hadn't been fond of me before the accident—I was her pesky little sister—and after, she could be downright hateful. The fact that I did everything for her only seemed to make her hate me more. She was mean and spiteful, with bouts of extreme rage when she struggled to do simple tasks, but I stuck it out and helped her for as long as she'd let me.

It did slowly get better. We spent many days on the floor, where I taught her to read, write, and talk. She wasn't saying much at first, but the books seemed to help—I had all my Dr. Suess books ready, and *Green Eggs and Ham* made her smile. I always reminded her to go to the toilet, and would take her with me to the bathroom when I went.

"Let's take a break and go potty," I would say. It really was like having a giant baby!

Despite her grumpiness, I became protective of her and cherished the eight months that I had her undivided attention.

Even though Brandy wasn't completely rehabilitated by the time the summer ended, she was able to start the new school year with me and Ivy. All those books had done their magic—her memories had come back and she was reading nearly at grade level. It was maybe even more of a miracle than my legs had been when they'd decided to grow straight after all.

Chapter 7

The Standoff

On the first day of fourth grade at Beverly Hills, as I walked into Mrs. James's classroom, I heard a boy yell out, "Look at Teener Wiener and her crazy hair!"

Not this again.

She intervened like a guardian angel would, saying, "Now, that's not nice. Fourth graders do not act that way." Coming to my rescue, she said, "Tina, come over here. Trey, you get to sit in the corner for five minutes."

To my surprise, she pulled me onto her lap and reached into her top drawer for a brush. As she began gently working through the knots in my fine curly mop, I marveled at the sensation. My mother's hurried attempts left my scalp throbbing or me running from her, which was why I often arrived at school with crazy hair.

Mrs. James tamed my curls into pigtails. Days turned into weeks, and she continued to fix my hair each morning.

My mother tended to pick her battles, but she also had her limits. At breakfast on any given day, my father might walk in with a black eye from one of my parents' fights gone out of control. He'd proceed to apologize to my mother, his voice filled with remorse and regret. He really sounded very sorry. Sometimes he would even stop drinking for a few days or even a whole week. But eventually, he would lose the fight to stay sober and drown himself in alcohol and it would start all over again.

He wasn't the only problem. Brandy's sharp tongue would ignite arguments between her and my mother on a regular basis. They fought about everything: clothes, make-up, cheerleading, boyfriends, you name it. She would relentlessly taunt my mother.

One day, it reached a breaking point.

Brandy had a permission slip that she needed signed, and my mother asked her to read it to her. Brandy shot back, "Read it yourself."

I was sitting there wondering what the problem was when she suddenly slapped Brandy across her cheek. Maybe my mother *couldn't* read, I thought, and Brandy had hurt her feelings on purpose. Their fights always seemed so stupid.

"I'm telling Daddy," Brandy declared, her voice filled with rage and triumph.

And that night, he arrived home, angry and drunk, already aware of what had transpired that day. I groaned—Brandy must have called him at work.

Without hesitation, he confronted my mother the moment he crossed the threshold. His face flushed with anger, he questioned her, yelling so loud I was sure the neighbors would hear. "Is it true?" he shouted. "Are you cheating on me?"

My mother gave us the look, and we ran to our closet. I huddled between Ivy and Brandy once inside. It was dark, but I could see light coming from the kitchen through the beads that hung in front of the closet as they swayed back and forth.

Apparently, Brandy had told my father she'd caught my mother talking to some guy on the phone.

My mother denied the accusation, responding, "No, Dub. What are you talking about?"

Once my eyes adjusted, I see the shadows of them moving.

"I'm not cheating on you," my mother was protesting. "That's ridiculous."

"I know you are," he said, as he pushed her up against the china cabinet that stood just outside our bedroom door.

I heard glass shatter and dishes fell to the ground. As my mother pleaded for him to let her go, she sounded strained and muffled. Time seemed to stand still as the commotion continued, until I could no longer hear her voice, only grunting and then a single loud thumping sound. I knew that was the sound of my mother's body hitting the floor—she was on the ground and he was choking her again.

I couldn't stand it anymore, and the need to help her was suddenly stronger than my fear. I darted out of the closet, Ivy's hand gripping my arm, holding me back, but I broke free.

The world seemed to be in slow motion as I entered the kitchen. My father had one knee on the floor, her body trapped between his legs where she lay on her back, and his huge hands were wrapped around her neck. Her head hung suspended a few inches above the floor—the way he was choking her made it shake and bounce a little. Her eyes were wide open, face cherry red, and she was barely moving.

Ivy came running up to where I stood, her footsteps echoing on the hardwood floors. My father didn't seem to notice us there— he just kept choking her.

"Please stop! You're killing her!" I screamed.

We both stood paralyzed, realizing he wasn't going to stop this time. I jumped on his back, my arms coiled around his neck, squeezing with all my might and screaming over and over for him to stop. Ivy joined in, screaming along with me. "Stop!" I yelled. "You're killing her!"

She wasn't moving at all anymore. I began punching him in the head.

Finally, he reached around to grab me, causing my mother's head to fall with a loud thud.

41

He wobbled as he stood up and shoved me into the dining room. I was on my butt, legs in front, both hands on the floor, and I slowly backed away. As our eyes locked, a silent understanding passed between us. I was the thing being hunted, the smaller and slower and weaker of the two animals that we were. And he was the hunter. His eyes told me so.

As I scrambled to my feet, I silently prayed for help.

He broke the standoff with an eerie grin and stumbled toward me. Closing in, he raised his hand, and I braced myself for the blow. Instead, he shoved me aside and headed to his bedroom.

THE REST of the night was a blur by the next morning, like my brain didn't want me to remember the horrible thing I had seen. But my mother didn't die after all, and was up making breakfast for us.

When I got home from school that day, Ivy went straight to our bedroom, and my mother went straight to hers, firmly closing both doors, the one that led to the kitchen and the other one that was closer to where I stood in the living room. I knew my father was in there with her, and I creeped up to her bedroom door to listen.

They were whispering, but I did hear my father tell my mother he'd taken Brandy to Aunt Colette and Uncle Chester's house and that she'd be staying in their bathhouse for a while.

That sure was weird. It didn't make sense that my sister wouldn't be living with us, even if she had caused some trouble. She was older than me, but still a kid. Couldn't my parents just make her behave?

Suddenly, my mother yelled, "She's a liar and I don't know what to do with her anymore." Then the bedroom door swung open. Thankfully, it was the door close to the kitchen.

I hurried to the sofa, opened my school folder, and shuffled papers around as though I had been doing my homework all the while. I could hear my mother in the kitchen, starting to make dinner. The pots and pans sounded a little louder than usual.

I sat on the sofa thinking it all through. Brandy leaving was a sudden change, but she had nearly gotten my mother killed with her lies, so maybe it was good for everyone to have some time to cool off. Everything had been a fight lately, and my father had stopped punishing Brandy and Ivy for being disrespectful to my mother, and that had just made things worse. Maybe things would go back to normal when Brandy came back?

AUNT COLETTE and Uncle Chester had a great marriage. In my eyes, it seemed perfect. A couple of years earlier, I'd asked them, "Do y'all ever fight? Because Mama and Daddy fight a lot."

Uncle Chester had quickly answered, "Only about your daddy, sweetheart."

Aunt Colette had responded, "Well, he's my brother, and you know he came back different after Korea."

"I know, Colette, but that was a very long time ago. He's bleeding us dry," he shot back.

"Blood is thicker than water, Chester," she had said heatedly. At this point, they were no longer talking to me.

That weekend, after my father nearly killed my mother, I sought refuge at Aunt Colette and Uncle Chester's house. My sister was already staying with them, and I liked it there, so I had asked my parents if I could go too.

My aunt and uncle's home felt safe, but was also pretty and elegant, with a long hallway with floor-to-ceiling glass windows on one side and four bedrooms on the other side. A bathroom at the end of the hallway opened to the den, which was close to the kitchen. It was an L-shaped design. From the hallway, you could see the swimming pool and the beautifully decorated patio with lush greenery all around. You could also see the black iron gate that led to the driveway, and I never liked to look at the gate very much, because it would remind me that, at some point, I would have to leave. I usually stayed in the first bedroom next to the bathroom, and I liked to pretend that it was my real room.

During that weekend, I was staying in my usual room, and on my way to the bathroom at night, I couldn't help but hear muffled voices coming from the kitchen.

It was my aunt and uncle, and it sounded important. I creeped up to the end of the hallway so I could eavesdrop.

"I saw a man go into the bathhouse with Brandy last night," Aunt Colette said.

"Did you know Dub was here this morning making coffee at six o'clock?" Uncle Chester said. I didn't hear a response, but Uncle Chester's cowboy boots hit the tile as he stood up to leave for work. In an angry voice that I'd never heard before, he said, "Colette, that's it. I know Dub's your brother, but this is not happening under my roof. It's flat out wrong and you know it."

I never saw Brandy, but supposedly she was living in the bathhouse. It sounded like my father had spent the night, but I never saw him either, and Uncle Chester was angry at him for making coffee at six in the morning. I didn't really understand why that was such a bad thing, except for maybe my father making coffee so early had woken Uncle Chester up.

Chapter 8

Decisions

About a week later, my father came into the kitchen, his footsteps heavy on the linoleum, and I could tell he wasn't there to have breakfast with us. He stood behind me with his hands on the back of my chair as he spoke. Ivy sat next to me, keeping her head down. I could smell the coffee brewing. "Well, your mother wants a divorce," he said. "Isn't that right, Jody?"

I shoveled another spoonful of cereal into my mouth, wondering what a divorce was. I'd heard some kids talking at school, that their parents had one, or were getting one, and it didn't sound good.

My mother kept her head down and didn't say a word. By the angry tone in my father's voice, I was sure now that it definitely wasn't a good thing. He walked out the door and slammed it as he was leaving.

"Girls, I'm going to get dressed. We're leaving in ten minutes," my mother said, walking away.

At recess that day, I ran over to my friends and said, "My parents are getting a divorce. Do you know what that is?" Later, I was called to the office by the principal, and he sternly told me to stay quiet about what was happening at home.

Until then, I had believed school was the best place to get answers. Apparently it wasn't.

THAT AFTERNOON, my mother picked me up from school and drove us to the beauty shop, where she had two clients waiting. On the way home, we didn't swing by the school to get Ivy, which we often did when she had to stay after for detention, or practice.

When I got home, as I put my backpack on the floor next to my bedroom door, I noticed through the beaded curtain that not many clothes were hanging in the closet and the many shoes that had covered the closet floor were gone. I quickly looked away. A sick feeling nagged at me, almost like I was about to panic, or throw up, but I pushed it down.

My mother was quieter than usual, but she started dinner at the regular time. I found it strange that we were the only ones in the house and Ivy's stuff was gone. Maybe that was why my mother was so quiet. I ran to the kitchen.

"Can I help?" I asked, hoping to ease the tension with my presence.

"Go play," she commented, without looking at me.

I could tell something wasn't right, and I did as she said, wandering into my bedroom. That's when I noticed clothes were missing from the closet. All of Ivy and Brandy's clothes. Our stereo and speakers were also gone. There was only one pillow on the king size bed I shared with my sisters.

Before I could ask my mother about all this, there was a knock at the door. I ran to open it, and she followed.

My father was standing there. Why hadn't he used his key?

"Hi, baby doll," he said to me.

My mother stepped forward when she heard his voice, putting her hands on my shoulders as he kept talking.

"Our renters moved out of the side apartment, so me and your sisters moved into it," my father explained, his voice slower and filled with much more patience than I was used to. "We will be living there, since your mother and I are getting a divorce," he said, motioning his arm to the left side of the house. "You can decide whether you want to live with me or stay here, but either way you will be close to me and your mother, since we are just a few feet away."

I wondered where I would sleep if I went to stay with him, since the side apartment was pretty small. I'd been in it—there was only a living room, and a bathroom, and a walk-in closet that connected to the kitchen.

I looked up at my mother, hoping for answers, but she was quiet.

"If you live with me, we'll go to your Aunt Colette's every weekend to swim and have cookouts."

I stayed silent.

"Dub, you need to leave. She's too young for this," my mother finally declared as she closed the door in his face. I stood there wondering why he didn't come inside the house.

As she returned to the kitchen, she said, "Have a seat. We're having spaghetti."

My mother motioned for me to sit at her beloved Louis XIV round white marble table. I devoured my food, but she picked at her plate, pushing the noodles around but barely eating anything. After a few minutes, she announced, "Your father isn't going to be living here anymore."

I kind of figured as much, since he had just invited me to live in his apartment. I nodded. "What about Ivy and Brandy? Are they going to live with us?"

"We'll see." She took a small bite of spaghetti. "Right now they are staying with your father, but I told them they can come visit anytime."

It felt weird to talk about visiting with my sisters. "Since they are right next door and we go to the same school, I'll see them a lot, right?"

"Yes, as much as you want to see them."

"Okay, Mama."

"Finish dinner so we can clean the kitchen, complete your homework, and get ready for bed."

A few days later, Ivy came to visit for a while. We played games and watched television shows like we used to. But I couldn't stop thinking about when she would leave.

"Ivy, why don't you want to live with us?" I finally asked. "You're always alone over there, anyway."

"Maybe when you're fifteen, you'll understand."

"Understand what? You should live with your family."

"Daddy is my family," she snapped back. "And Brandy is there too."

"But I'm lonely, and I miss you." I held back my tears. Big girls didn't cry, so I needed to be brave.

"You don't get it. Mama treats you different from how she treats me and Brandy."

"That's because you talk back to her all the time. And you won't go to school."

"Whatever."

A FEW WEEKS LATER, Ivy was over visiting again, and something happened. She popped off at my mother, and I knew right that second I would never forget what happened next. I didn't catch exactly what it was that Ivy said, but what I did see was my mother instantly turning a shade of red I had never seen before. In a fit of anger, my mother's hand closed tightly around a sharp screwdriver that sat atop the washer, and she chased Ivy around the house and out the front door.

I'd always had the feeling there were secrets, things I didn't know about, but today was different. Sure, Ivy popped off and was sarcastic to my mother every now and then, but I'd never seen this type of aggressive behavior from my mother toward Ivy.

What could Ivy have said that had made my mother chase her with a sharp metal object?

FROM THEN ON, my mother and I fell into a solitary routine. The sight of my school as her car pulled away from the curb each morning signaled the start of another long day for me. I would rush into the building and head straight upstairs to find Ivy before class started for her, but sometimes I would come across Brandy instead. Neither of them was excited to see me and would urge me to go to class. Still, I went up to look for them every morning.

At the end of the school day, I'd crawl into the front seat of my mother's Chrysler and burst into tears. After explaining what had happened, she would say something like, "Your sisters love you, but being in high school is hard."

It didn't make me feel any better.

She would then drive us to the beauty shop, though often times we'd stop at the church to light a candle and pray first. At the shop, I stayed busy and out of the way while I waited for her to finish up. Back at home, my mother would begin cooking dinner. If she was in a good mood, she would sing and dance too, and I'd join in, but most days, I sat at the table working on homework, or coloring. Sometimes I could hear my sisters talking, laughing, and playing music through the wall. I wondered if they hated me, my mother, or both of us. Sometimes I gave up on being a big girl and would cry.

I struggled, torn between my mother and my sisters. I paced the floor every Friday after school, the sound of my footsteps echoing through the silent house. I watched the clock, wondering when my father was going to come knocking at the door and, if he did, whether I should go with him to my aunt and uncle's house or stay home with my mother. My chest tightened as I wondered if she would be okay without me, or if she would feel sad.

When I'd open the door to find my father standing on the other side, I'd have to make the choice. "You don't have to come," he'd say, "but we're going to your Aunt Colette's."

I felt stretched in two directions, a rubber band about to snap. I'd look to my mother, who would release me from my burden with her words. "It's okay, honey. Go be with your sisters; they love you." The warmth of her voice soothed my inner conflict.

On the days my father came and picked me up, I saw little of him once we arrived at my aunt and uncle's house. He was always off somewhere, doing something. I wondered if he even cared about spending time with me or if he just didn't want me with my mother. I'd heard her say something like that on the phone to somebody.

It was like my mother and father were playing a game, or having a contest, but I couldn't see the fun in it, and it didn't seem like a game you could win.

On the weekends that I had fun with my sisters, away from my mother, a huge blanket of guilt would wrap itself around me. The conflicting emotions would swirl within me as I questioned my loyalty to my mother, but also my sisters that I no longer lived with. I felt like a traitor on both sides.

Chapter 9

Does Mama Know

C hristmas was approaching, and I settled into a wonderful fantasyland where I again began to dream that our family would live together again, that my sisters would love me, and that my parents, reunited by some miracle, adored each other. But that all changed one evening when my father came home.

"Pack your things. We're moving to Garland," my father announced a week before Christmas. I had just moved in with him, Brandy, and Ivy a few days before.

"Today?" I asked.

"Yes, right now," he said, waving me toward the door impatiently.

"Does . . . does Mama know?" I asked, my voice quivering. His eyes met mine, and I knew better than to question him any further. Shoulders slumping, I headed toward my room, a closet off the kitchen where I had been sleeping beside Ivy on a twin mattress. As I stuffed my few things into a suitcase, the last conversation I'd had with my mother played through my mind.

I remembered sitting on the tan suede sofa, picking nervously at the fabric as my Mama explained why she thought it would be better for me to go live with my sisters temporarily. "I know you miss them, and they miss you. It will give you all a chance to spend some time together. Only for a little while—just until I can get on my feet," she said. "I love you very much, but this is best for now. As she turned quickly to look out the window, I was pretty sure I saw tears gathered in the corners of her eyes. But when she turned back to face me, all trace of them was gone. "Besides, *mija,* you'll only be right next door," she whispered.

"But you'll be all alone," I said, my own tears streaming down my face.

"I'm never alone—God is always with me," she said, holding me close. A moment later, she pulled away, held both of my shoulders, gazed into my eyes and said, "Never forget that God is always with you too, no matter what."

I clung to her fiercely, breathing in her Estée Lauder perfume as she gently stroked my hair.

"And as soon as I get back from seeing my family in El Paso, you can come right over here anytime," she said, smiling.

My eyes got big. "You have family in El Paso?"

"Yes, don't worry—you're going to meet them real soon."

I felt relieved, and hopeful, knowing she'd come back for me.

Ivy's voice pierced through the air, breaking me out of my daydream and back into the moment. "Tina, we're leaving—let's go," she said.

Clutching my favorite baby doll tightly, I followed my sisters out to the car.

Half an hour later, we arrived at a run-down building in Garland. It was dark and cold, and I was tired. My father ushered the three of us into a cramped two-bedroom apartment. As I flipped on the kitchen light, roaches scattered. *Not this again*, I thought.

I turned to look for my father, only to find him gone. I had no clue why he had moved us to this awful apartment, which had ugly brown shag carpet, dingy-looking walls, and a smell that suggested animals had just moved out.

He had told me I'd be close to Mama's house, and I could see her anytime I wanted if I lived with him. *How is that going to work now?* I wondered.

There were already two twin beds in the bedroom Ivy and me were to share , one against each wall. My father had his own room with a big bed, and I guessed that Brandy was going to sleep on the sofa.

INITIALLY, it felt as though Ivy and I were the only ones living there. My father and Brandy treated the apartment like a crash pad, only stopping by to sleep and shower.

In a lot of ways, Ivy became more like my mother than my sister. When necessary, she would get us groceries. She'd buy Cokes, Kool-Aid, bread, peanut butter, jelly, bologna, and cheese. Most days, we'd have sandwiches. Occasionally, Ivy would transform the bologna into a sizzling delight. And if we had a little extra money, she'd concoct mac-n-cheese with the added zest of hot dogs. But I really missed Mama's enchiladas and spaghetti.

We didn't have a phone for the first few weeks in Garland. When we finally got one, Ivy would dial for me so I could talk with my mother several times a week. At the end of each call, my mother would end by saying, "I love you very much and I'm going to see you real soon."

I would cry at the end of each call, clutching the cord while Ivy struggled to put the phone back into its cradle. Maybe that was why, over time, the calls became less frequent—Ivy didn't want to hear me break down afterward. It seemed to upset everyone if I mentioned Mama, so I stopped asking about her, and it made me sad to think about her, so I tried not to.

My father only talked about his new girlfriends. A month after the move, he introduced me to a lady named Wendy, who was

Aunt Colette's friend. He'd always been quite the charmer—it was what everyone said, anyway—and he'd already convinced this lady to marry him. However, soon after I met her, she met the mean Dub, and I never saw her again.

FOLLOWING CHRISTMAS BREAK, Ivy and I started attending school. My father never asked if we went or not, perhaps because he didn't see the point—he would always say he was doing just fine having only gone through sixth grade. Brandy, who had dropped out of high school before we moved, had decided to get a job and was rarely at home.

The first few weeks, Ivy walked me to school, and it was fun. We'd take a shortcut through the creek behind the apartment. It was like a hiking adventure, and it took less time to get there too. But it didn't take long before I caught Ivy smoking weed. After I questioned her about it, she started distancing herself from me.

One cold, rainy morning, Ivy refused to wake up. I nudged her gently, but she growled at me, saying, "Go away." I shook her again, more urgently this time—I was barely ten years old and not ready to go alone. She rolled over, her eyes barely open, and snapped, "It's time for you to grow up. You can walk yourself to school."

I stood there staring at her for a moment. I thought about the creek I'd have to cross by myself. It would be terrifying, but I had no choice—I had to go to school.

Even though I was afraid, I went, and continued to do that every day thereafter. And at some point, it stopped being scary.

I settled into a new normal for a few months. My father and Brandy were hardly ever home, and when they were, we never saw them. They stopped in every few days. Ivy had stopped going to school and slept all day. I kept going to school because I didn't know what else to do.

As the months dragged on, Brandy and my father fought more and more about where'd she'd been and with whom. One day, I came home from school and went straight to my room to find Ivy sleeping. I sat on my bed, going through my folders from school. The house was quiet, but then I thought I heard Brandy giggle. I perked up from my bed and put my ear against the wall and heard a muffled male voice. I walked over to Ivy's bed and shook her.

"Ivy, wake up," I whispered.

She snapped back, "What do you want? I'm tired."

"I think Brandy is home and in Daddy's room with a man."

Ivy jumped to her feet. "Stay here," she said, tiptoeing out of our room. I followed her anyway, but stopped at the edge of our door and peeked around the corner to watch her. She was standing in the hallway, close to my father's bedroom. She wasn't there long before she hurried back, closed our door, turned on the radio, and said, "Find your coloring books and color." Her face had turned white, and she sat on the side of her bed staring at the wall for a few minutes before lying down.

Ivy had been staring at the ceiling for at least an hour when I heard the front door open, and my father's voice. I perked up, "Is Daddy home?"

"No, he's leaving," she barked.

By the way Ivy was acting, I knew something wasn't right, but I also knew I'd better stop asking questions, at least for now.

The next day, we were lounging in our room and Ivy jumped up from her bed and said, "I want to know what's going on." She went to my father's room and opened the door. I followed her, my heart beating fast, wondering what we were doing. She bent down to look under the bed, and so did I.

We found some magazines with naked men and women in them. They weren't the kind of magazines I'd seen before.

Ivy took a deep breath, like you would if something scared you. "Let's go," she said, gently pushing me forward with her hand on my back. I could feel it trembling. That made me nervous—if Ivy was scared, I should be too.

She raced to the phone, called my mother, and I heard her tell my mother that there were dirty magazines under my father's bed, and that Brandy has been sleeping in his room with the door closed. I couldn't hear what my mother was saying, but Ivy had tears coming to her eyes. She smacked the bed with her hand and said, "I don't understand why you can't do anything to help us." Then she slammed the phone down.

"What did she say?" I said, my frustration matching Ivy's, even though I had no idea what was happening.

"Mama said to call Aunt Colette because she couldn't do anything." Ivy stopped her tears, wiping them away roughly.

"Well, call her then," I said.

Ivy tried, but couldn't reach Aunt Colette. She called her daughter Tara and, after she answered, Ivy told her what we'd found, and how she thought Brandy had been sleeping in his room with the door locked.

"I'm calling my mama," Tara said before they ended the call.

A few minutes later, Tara called back. "Pack your bags—I'm on my way."

She picked us up and drove us to Aunt Colette's house.

Ivy and I sat in the game room with Aunt Colette. Ivy recounted the events about daddy and Brandy being in his room and told her how we'd frequently been all alone in the apartment for days at a time.

Aunt Colette responded with, "You must be confused. You need to tell your mama about this." She put her head in her hands.

"I'm not confused, and Mama said she couldn't do anything and that we needed to tell you because only you could help," Ivy replied, a little too sharply.

The next thing that happened surprised me more than the dirty magazines had.

"Tara, you have to take them home," Aunt Colette said, her voice angry. "I can't handle this."

As we walked out the door, those memories of being Aunt Colette's pride and joy just disappeared.

The ride home was quiet. Tara stopped the car in front of the apartment to let us out. "Girls," she said, "I'm so sorry, but I'm going to talk to my daddy when he gets home from work—this isn't over. You know how Mama is. She can't handle anything."

I hadn't known that, but now I did.

Ivy was crying, and she slammed the car door when she got out. I didn't understand what was happening, but I knew it wasn't good. Tara and Aunt Colette seemed upset too—I guessed this was because they couldn't do anything to help us. If something could be done, Uncle Chester would do it, but it didn't seem like Ivy agreed. She was cooking mac-n-cheese and banging things around, instead of listening to music, which was her usual routine. I stayed out of her way for the rest of the day.

A FEW WEEKS LATER, my father introduced me to a lady named Pam. I thought surely this one wouldn't last either, but a few days later, they announced their engagement. It all happened so quickly. Pam had a daughter, Lena. She was short like Ivy, but rounder than her, and dressed like a cowgirl. Lena was fifteen and Ivy was sixteen. The entire family seemed excited and happy, so I just went along. Next thing I knew, they were married, and we were all moving to San Angelo.

I wondered if Mama knew we were moving again and when she would be coming back for me. I hadn't seen her since we'd moved to Garland and I couldn't remember the last time I'd spoken to her. *How will she know where to find me?* I thought.

Chapter 10

Chickens

Ivy and I had to ride with Pam and Lena to Harriet, Texas, the tiny town outside of San Angelo where it turned out we would actually be moving. It was gloomy and a tad chilly when we left Dallas late in the afternoon. During the trip, I put my mother out of my mind and tried to have fun. I'd never been on a long road trip before and stopping at the gas stations for cokes and chips made it all the more an adventure. To pass the time, we played the license-plate and I-spy games.

Five hours later, I saw a sign that said "Welcome to Harriet" before we turned on a country road that led to where we'd be staying. Pam's brother was a dairy farmer, and we were apparently going to live with him. As I stepped into the house, I turned to look over my shoulder out the front door—there was nothing for miles but fields of grass stretching for as far as I could see.

Pam explained that her brother left the house early in the mornings and returned in the evenings at dusk. When he got home that evening, he didn't say much to me at all and I didn't to him either.

The day after we arrived, Ivy and Lena had gone gallivanting, as

Pam called it, and I was sitting on the floor in my new bedroom playing with my Barbies. I heard footsteps on the hardwood floors coming down the hallway and, when they stopped, I could feel Pam standing there.

"Did you know me and your daddy were married before you were born?" she said.

I shook my head no.

"Yeah, your mama split me and your daddy up."

I focused my eyes on her pink muumuu and thick mid-section, wondering why my father would ever pick this woman over my mother. Thankfully, Ivy and Lena walked in the door and interrupted us. Ivy went straight to her room for a nap. Pam told Lena to go feed the chickens while she cooked dinner. I had been stuck in the house all day, so I begged Lena to take me with her. Luckily, she said yes—I was excited to ride down to the coop in Pam's truck.

Lena showed me how to feed the chickens and warned me that the turkey could be mean and to avoid him.

We had a good time.

THE FOLLOWING DAY WAS A MONDAY, and I rode the bus to my new school—I'd never done that before. I was scared, but Pam said it would be good for me to learn some independence and pushed me out the front door. "Just wait near the street and get on when it pulls up and opens the door," Pam yelled from inside the house. So, I dutifully stood out at the end of the long driveway, willing myself not to cry as Ivy and Lena drove by me on their way to school in Lena's car. I wondered why they couldn't just take me, but I wasn't brave enough to ask.

The bus sped toward me, and I couldn't tell if the driver had noticed me. The brakes squealed, and the vehicle jerked to a halt right in front of me. A sharp *whoosh* sounded as the door swung open, and I hesitated. The driver leaned out, his voice gruff. "Come on in," he said, then asked, "Are you Pam's niece?"

I just nodded—far easier than explaining.

Grabbing the metal bar, I took three giant steps and found myself under the gaze of a busload of curious kids. I made my way to the back, weaving through the seats until I spotted an empty one. I slid into the seat by the window just as the bus jolted forward. Holding onto the seat in front of me, I braced myself, as I bounced around for an hour.

When I finally reached the school office, they greeted me by name, as if they'd been expecting me. A kind lady escorted me to the fourth-grade classroom. As I entered, I couldn't help but notice how most of the kids were dressed in blue jeans—even the girls. My pink frilly dress and the stiff, white patent leather Mary Janes felt out of place. At lunch, I sat alone, my gaze fixed on my food, careful not to make eye contact with anyone. I stared at the clock in the classroom, waiting for three o'clock.

When the bell rang, panic surged through me. I couldn't remember where to find the bus, and my heart was thumping in my chest. As I stood still, I heard one boy that I recognized from the morning shout to his friend, "Hurry, we're going to miss the bus!" Without thinking, I ran to catch up to them. By the time I reached the line of buses, sweat dripped down my forehead and I was gasping for air. But I was also relieved to be on my way home.

The ride home felt like a repeat of the morning, except this time the noise was piercing. The kids around me laughed and shouted nonstop. Not knowing anyone, I stayed quiet, staring out the window. When I stepped off the bus, I felt a little woozy and not steady on my feet. I shuffled into the house and asked Pam for a snack in an attempt to settle my stomach. After I'd had a glass of orange juice and a few crackers, she said, "Why don't you walk down the road to the next house. Maybe Shelly is there, visiting her grandmother. She's about your age—maybe ten or eleven." It sounded like a great way to cure my boredom, so I agreed.

I started down the gravel road, kicking at big rocks and cans, just like I used to when I played soccer. I really missed playing, and

I missed my friends too. As I approached the driveway, I didn't see a car, but what I did see stopped me in my tracks. It was a ginormous dog that reminded me of Barry from *Barry of the Great St Bernard*, movie I'd seen. His white nose stood out against his black eyes, and brown ears flopped around as he moved. He was adorable, but also ginormous—probably as tall as my father when he put his legs on top of the chain link fence. My heart fluttered at the sight of him.

Since no one was around, I opened the gate to go in and play with him, but he got very excited and began twisting and jumping around. He pounced on me over and over—I felt like I was a little mouse, and this big giant was going to crush me. I somehow didn't fall to the ground, but I was screaming for him to stop and trying to get out of the gate while also not letting him out. I gave up after a few seconds and he pushed past me and took off running to who knew where. I was a little shaken up, but dusted myself off and walked home, vowing I would never tell a soul.

The next day after school, I'd complained to Pam that I was bored—for the second or third time, at that point. Out of frustration, she'd thrown me the keys to the big Ford truck and told me to go feed the chickens. I was surprised—my father had let me drive on his lap a lot, but no one had trusted me to take a car out on my own.

This was *huge*.

I went out to the truck and realized I couldn't reach the pedals. I went back inside to tell Pam, and she told me to take a pillow and sit on it. So I did. I still couldn't reach the pedals and I wondered how adding a pillow would have solved that. I ended up being able to reach if I half-stood-half-sat at the very edge of the bench seat.

When I got to the enclosure where the chickens were kept, I saw the turkey that Lena had warned me about. He didn't like me very much—I thought he was running at me for food at first, but it turned into a nasty chase that almost had me in tears. He was definitely trying to eat me!

Tina Montoya

On my way back from feeding the chickens, driving the bumpy half mile down the dirt road, I sniffed at the air—the smell of cow manure filled it, and the sun was in my line of sight, disappearing into the clouds. The sky was orange and purple. I'd never seen anything like that before. The view was so beautiful that it distracted me, so much so that I had stopped pressing down on the gas pedal. Watching the sky change colors reminded me of my mother—I wasn't sure why. I took in a deep breath and imagined that she and I were watching it together, but in two different locations. I heard a car honking and I quickly stepped on the gas and continued down the road.

Chapter 11

The ICU

I was in the living room watching television the night I learned my mother had been shot. We'd only been in Harriet three days, and I was settling in for the night after getting back from feeding the chickens at a neighbor's nearby property.

It was just before dark when the telephone rang. Pam yelled, "Girls, your daddy is on the phone!"

The plan had been for Ivy and me to move in with Pam and start school, while my father stayed behind to close his business. Ivy and I were not happy about being there with this strange lady we didn't know, who plastered her short, black-dyed hair to her head until it resembled an upside-down bowl and wasn't especially nice to us. Why were we living with her and not our mother again? I was hoping to get some answers when my father joined us.

Walking into Pam's bedroom, I found her lying in her twin bed, the novel she'd been reading now on the nightstand next to the base of the telephone. She gripped the receiver in her hand.

I sat down on the mattress. Pam quickly straightened, sitting up, and sucked in her breath. Her face turned pale—something wasn't right.

"You need to tell them," she exclaimed, passing the phone to Ivy, who stood next to me.

Ivy was quiet at first. Then, her voice trembling with anger, she yelled, "You finally did it! I know you did!" She handed the phone back to Pam and ran to our bedroom. A moment later, I could hear her smashing and banging things around.

"Dub, here's Tina," Pam said nervously.

I held the phone to my ear.

"Hello, Tina. Are you there?" It was my father. He sounded strange, and I immediately felt uneasy.

"Yes, Daddy, I'm here."

"Your mother shot herself," he said matter-of-factly. "There's nothing we can do." I handed the phone back to Pam without saying a word, wondering what it all meant.

"We are going *tonight*!" Ivy screamed from her room.

"I'm putting the girls on the bus this evening," Pam said with urgency. "Pick them up tomorrow morning at the Greyhound station in Dallas. Let them visit their mother before it's too late." As she slammed the phone onto its cradle, I jumped. "Your father wants you to stay here, but I'm sending you. Hurry, go grab your things."

I rushed to our bedroom. The sight of clothes scattered across the floor added to the chaos. "What should I pack?" I asked Ivy.

"We are *never* coming back here. Take what you can," she said, her voice filled with determination.

Overwhelmed, I walked out to the living area. It seemed as though the walls were closing in on me, the room spinning. I held onto the wall and slid to the couch, feeling nauseous. Was my mother going to die? Why did this happen?

Was it because I left her?

"Let's go—we're leaving," Ivy said, her voice bringing me back into the moment. I noticed her carrying a duffle bag and walking out to Pam's truck. The sight of her ready to leave had me on my feet.

I hurried to my room, opened my little purple suitcase, and quickly threw in a couple of outfits and grabbed my Pink Panther. A few minutes later, Pam was driving us down the pitch-black country road to downtown San Angelo.

Pam left us at the busy Greyhound station. As we got on the bus to Dallas, I settled into a seat, the coolness of the leather giving me chills. I held my stuffed animal tightly to stay warm. During the long trip, I was confused. Ivy didn't say much to me. She sat fuming, with her arms crossed. Every so often she would shake her head and mumble, "He did it—he shot her. I know it."

It was eight o'clock the next morning by the time we arrived in downtown Dallas. The warmth and brightness of the sun hit me as we walked off the bus. We waited for several minutes, wondering who would come for us, and then we noticed our cousin Sam turning into the parking lot. I climbed into the back seat.

I saw a white sign with red letters that read Parkland Hospital. Sam dropped us on the curb at the door. I gathered my Coke and my honeybun leftovers and we waited there for him to park the car.

The large glass doors slid open as we grew near them, and I trailed behind Ivy and Sam. Upon reaching the elevator, I felt nauseous. Stepping out onto the second floor, I could see my father standing in the hallway, in front of the room I guessed my mother must be in. As I approached him, I noticed Brandy was standing next to him.

Ivy walked into the room and I started to follow her. When the nurse that was in the room made eye contact with me, she held up her hand, indicating for me to stop, and said, "Kids under twelve are not allowed, and Jody can only have one visitor at a time."

Well, then, I thought, *why are Brandy and Daddy standing at the door if she can only have one visitor?*

My father pointed to the chairs in the cold, empty hallway. Sam had left to smoke a cigarette. I sat alone, struggling to eat the rest of my honey bun.

A few minutes later, Ivy walked out and I saw an old couple

walk in. It was Francis and Virgil—my mother's best friends, who I hadn't seen in a long time. My father poked his head out the door and whispered, "Hurry—the nurse is gone."

I ran to him, and a second wave of nausea washed over me as I walked into the room—an awful smell had hit me in the face, and suddenly my mind was consumed by memories of my trips to Scottish Rite.

The nurse returned once I stepped inside, but I kept walking toward my mother's bed. "How old is she?" she asked with her hands on her hips.

"She's twelve," my father replied confidently. I had recently turned ten four months earlier and thought for sure she was going to throw me out.

"You've got five minutes, and that's it, but they need to leave," she said, pointing at Francis and Virgil.

My mother lay slightly propped up on the bed, with wires connecting her to monitors that were softly beeping. Her stomach area was covered with a blanket. The tube in her mouth prevented her from talking and made a swooshing noise.

My father came over, stood behind me and grabbed her hand. "We're getting back together, Tina," he said nervously.

My mother's eyes met mine. Hers were glassy and red, filled with the same look I'd seen the last time my father had choked her. She began sobbing uncontrollably, and the machines beeped louder and faster.

The nurse rushed in. "Everyone out. Now!" she yelled.

As I ran from her room, everything was spinning. I had only gone a short distance into the hallway when I fell to the floor and spewed the honey bun and coke everywhere.

I was on my hands and knees, my palms pressing into the cold tile. I heard the ding of the elevator door. A woman stepped out—Mama? I turned to look back at the hospital room and then back at the woman. My body shaking, and with everything fuzzy feeling, I tried to stand up but slipped on the vomit and fell onto my butt.

As the out-of-focus woman approached me, I was pulled from the floor by someone grabbing my left arm.

It was Ivy. "I can't believe you," she said. "It's Aunt Delia. Come on, let's go."

The woman I had seen was evidently my mother's sister. She looked like her twin.

Ivy and I went looking for Sam downstairs. He drove us to Aunt Colette's house, where we waited every day for updates. We didn't visit the hospital again, and nobody talked about Mama except Uncle Chester. Fourteen days later, he sat me on his lap and said, "Your mother died today."

I began to cry.

He continued. "I know this is hard. I lost my mother when I was six years old, but you don't have to worry about anything. Your Aunt Colette and I love you as if you were our own child. I'm not going to let anyone hurt you and I'll never leave you. We're going to make sure your mother has a nice funeral."

A FEW DAYS LATER, I was at my mother's funeral, the overwhelming sense of being a character in a television show making everything feel even more unreal. As I entered the room, I noticed a cream-colored casket with my mother inside. We walked down the center aisle to the front pew on the left. There were pretty floral arrangements all around. Mama loved flowers, and I wondered if she was happy. My dress was tight—I had almost outgrown it—but I knew she would not have approved of pants, so I made the best of it, struggling now and then to catch a full breath.

After "Amazing Grace" had played from the ceiling, my father gripped my hand, leading me toward her casket. He patted me on the back as we stood before the body that didn't look anything like hers. She was bigger, swollen looking, and her skin looked orange, like the spray tanner Brandy had once used. My father said something to me, but I couldn't understand his words. I felt as if I were outside myself.

Walking back to my seat, I could see a dozen people on the left side of the room that I did not recognize. They were dark-complected and spoke a language other than English. I heard whispers of "that's Jody's family from El Paso," and, looking over at them, wondered which one was my brother. My mother had told me I had a brother during our last conversation. The room was filled with an unspoken tension between my mother's family and my father's family. My father's face was very serious the entire time, and he didn't shed a single tear for my mother. But I didn't cry either, reminding myself over and over again that big girls didn't do that.

Chapter 12

Aftermath

After my mother died, we moved into her house. Sitting on the sofa, memories of us together flooded my mind. It was the same spot where my mother held me during our last conversation. Looking down at the floor, I tried to understand all the things that had happened in the last month. My mother had supposedly borrowed my father's gun a few weeks before, then called my father at the store while he was working, and begged him to come over. She then used his .38 revolver, loaded with hollow-point bullets, to shoot herself in the stomach, because he wouldn't agree to go back to her.

That was the story my father had sold to the police, but I wasn't buying it. I had eavesdropped on many conversations between family members, and I had heard that Brandy was sleeping in the small apartment in the back of the store where my father had been working that day, before he left to go see my mother. I just didn't get it, and I needed to understand.

There were other facts that made it confusing. I knew that Ivy, who seemed fine with my father before my mother died, hated him now and had accused him of killing her several times when he came home drunk. "I know you did it—just admit it," she would say. His only response was always a smirk.

On one of these occasions, in a voice filled with self-pity, he had asked me, "Do you believe I killed your mother?" I shrugged my shoulders and lowered my eyes, fearing the consequences of telling the truth. My answer only seemed to anger him, but he didn't follow his strange question up with anything—he didn't say he didn't kill her and he said absolutely nothing to make me feel any better.

He never talked about that day, or explained what had happened. It was clear to me that I would never know the whole truth. I had to accept that and focus on surviving.

With summer now here, there were no rules or routines to follow. My father came home less and less. We could go several days without seeing him. Brandy and Ivy took advantage of his absence and threw wild parties at the house several nights a week. My sisters told me to stay in my room, but I couldn't help but come out and mingle. I relished in the ability to hang out with my sisters' friends and forget that I was their pesky sister.

Brandy left for a few weeks and the parties ended.

One night, Brandy finally came home. The three of us were lounging in the living room watching television when my father stumbled in the door. He sat on the couch to join us as if we'd never skipped a beat, not even asking where Brandy had been all this time.

As if she'd been waiting for him to return home, Brandy stood, turned off the television, and said, "I have an announcement." We looked at her. "I'm moving out to live with Bob," she declared. And without hesitation, she grabbed me by the wrist, pulling me from the sofa and shoving me behind her. "I'm taking Tina with me," she said, pointing at my father. "You aren't going to do to her what you did to me!"

Despite the intense chaos of the moment, I felt a swell of affection—my sister actually *did* care about me.

My father's face turned three shades of red, and at first, he didn't move a muscle—he stared at Brandy. And then, in a swift motion, he sprang to his feet, grabbing Ivy and me by the arms, forcefully pushing us out through the front door. He slammed the door and locked it. We could hear him screaming at Brandy.

Ivy and I stood side by side, peering through the large plate-glass window beside the front door. My heart raced as I took in the horrifying sight. My father's left hand clenched tightly around Brandy's delicate throat, his fingers digging into her skin as he had done so many times to my mother. He punched her in the stomach with his right.

Was he going to kill her?

She kicked and screamed like a wild donkey, trying to get away, before he flung her hundred-pound body across the room. The way she hit the wall and slid to the floor like a rag doll reminded me of a cartoon. Brandy crawled to the front door and grabbed the baseball bat and began swinging for his knees. But she didn't have the strength to do him any harm.

Something nudged me into motion, and I hit Ivy on the arm. "Ivy, we have to do something!" I yelled, my voice trembling. I was terrified, but something had to be done, and now.

She stayed frozen, eyes wide, and unable to speak.

I grabbed the nearest thing to me, a white plastic five-gallon bucket, and swung it as hard as I could at the window. It shattered. And luckily for Brandy, it shocked my father as much as it shocked me. During his moment of hesitation, Brandy swung the bat, hitting him hard in the stomach, and air whooshed out of him as he fell to the ground. Without hesitation, she dashed to the front door and unlocked it.

I stood by the door and kept watch over my father, my heart thumping into my throat. He cried in agony on the floor while Brandy and Ivy rushed around the house, gathering what they could. Ivy grabbed the keys to the Chrysler and rushed outside.

I could hear the engine revving and Ivy yelling for us to hurry.

Brandy was scurrying frantically around the house, trying to find something.

"Just forget it," I said. My father was catching his breath and we needed to book it.

"Found it!" she finally yelled, as she bolted for the door, her makeup bag clutched in her hand.

I took off running, Brandy at my heels, and jumped into the back seat. I saw my father come out of the house right before Brandy closed the passenger-side door. Ivy shifted into drive when my father ran in front of the car.

Filled with panic, Brandy and I shouted, "Hit him, Ivy—hit him!"

As Ivy floored it, my father either jumped onto the hood or the car catapulted him onto it before he slid off the side onto the ground. Ivy backed up a little and turned the steering wheel to the right to drive around him.

We were all shaken, none of us having any idea what to do next. Brandy broke the silence, and she ordered Ivy to find a payphone. Ten blocks from our house, Ivy slowed to a stop.

Brandy ran to the pay phone to call her boyfriend, Robert.

Robert came for us, and we left the car on the side of the road. We slept at his house that night.

The next morning, the sun rose, and I saw a golden glow out his kitchen window. As he prepared breakfast for us, the aroma of sizzling bacon filled the air, mixing with the comforting smell of brewed coffee. Brandy, her eyes filled with tears, shared her news with us—she was pregnant.

"I'll never go back to that house again," she said as she grabbed Bob's hand. "Please help us," she pleaded in a soft voice.

"You guys can't stay here," he said to me and Ivy. "I'm sorry."

Brandy, standing behind him, mouthed, "I'm sorry."

As Bob drove us back home, my hands trembled, and my heart was pounding in my chest. The morning breeze blew the curtains —the broken window remained uncovered. I hesitated, not wanting to step a foot inside. I had to force myself to climb the stairs and follow Ivy through the screen door. And there on the sofa was my father, his body sprawled out, surrounded by broken glass. The bat and the bucket were right where we'd left them.

Ivy and I continued our day, ignoring the mess in the living room. By the time my father stirred, we had already showered and eaten lunch. I was hoping he wouldn't recall what had happened. We sat at the kitchen table as he rose from the sofa and showered. Without a word, he left the house.

Ivy and I couldn't help but giggle, a release of the tension that had been building. The thought of my father waking up hungover, his body aching, and the house in disarray, without any recollection of the chaos, brought a sense of twisted satisfaction.

"Serves him right," Ivy said, when our fits of laughter had subsided.

"It sure does," I said.

My father never mentioned the incident, nor did he acknowledge Brandy's long absence.

With Brandy gone, Ivy and I grew closer than ever. It felt as if we were a united team, facing the world together. My father was rarely home. Every three or four days, he'd pop by for a shower and a change of clothes. Ivy enrolled me in fifth grade and ensured we had food. If we ran out of food, she was the one who boldly confronted my father. And, in response, he would leave behind a small sum of money for groceries before disappearing back into his world of partying. He was working at Uncle Chester's store again, and we'd usually drive there first. If we'd had a telephone, it sure would have been easier to call, but at least he left us the green Dodge Demon that Ivy had to start with a screwdriver. If he wasn't at the store working or sleeping in its attached apartment, then Cookie's was the next stop.

Ivy would turn up the radio, and we'd sing our hearts out during the thirty-minute drive to Cookie's, a dark, dingy, hole-in-the-wall bar. If we couldn't find my father there, we might find

Uncle Jack picking his guitar, which was the next best thing. But if we couldn't find either of them, sometimes the regulars would throw us a five or ten dollar bill for gas or food.

As we pulled into the parking lot, if our windows were down, we would sometimes hear Uncle Jack singing. Ivy and I would look at each other and smile knowing we'd hit the jackpot that day.

We'd guzzle down burgers and sodas along with black smoke that filled the bar. With our bellies full, it was time to earn our keep by singing with Uncle Jack. Songs like *You're the Reason God Made Oklahoma*, by David Frizzell and Shelly West, and *Elvira* by the Oak Ridge Boys. A few hours later, the tips would pile up, and I'd take a nap in a corner booth while Ivy and Uncle Jack kept on singing, sometimes until closing.

SHORTLY AFTER I TURNED ELEVEN, my father announced we were moving out of my mother's house and into Aunt Colette's rental house in Pleasant Grove, effective immediately. Ivy and I ran around frantically, grabbing whatever we needed.

The new house meant a new school district, and even though it was only February, my father said I'd start fresh in the fall. It didn't take long for me to understand the real reason I wasn't going to school. I had to take care of my father's girlfriend's baby and Ivy's friend's baby. Instead of a fifth grade filled with schoolwork and friends, I lived in a revolving door of diapers, bottles, and screaming infants.

Ivy spent more and more time partying with her friends, seeking solace and respite from the weight of our reality. I didn't see her much at all, but I'd heard she had an older girlfriend that had been telling her she needed to clean herself up and get her diploma. But that wasn't going to happen while living under my father's roof, and, to compound things, since she'd just turned eighteen, she was no longer a minor and free from my father's control.

I guess, sometime after the funeral, she had reconnected with my half-brother, who lived in El Paso, and he invited her to live with him and his wife. She was leaving Pleasant Grove. It seemed like my whole world—or what was left of it—was crumbling around me as I sat on the floor sobbing, begging her to take me with her.

As she opened the door, without turning back to look at me, she gave me some parting words. "I know you're only eleven, but you have to find your own way now. I need to go live my own life."

With Ivy gone and my father no longer dating the lady with a baby, I was mostly alone now. I tried to stay busy, desperately clinging to any sense of normalcy. I'd plan a schedule for everything —my meals, television shows, showering, exercise, and bedtime. Each day, I woke up and started my routine all over again, hoping for something, anything, to break up the monotony. And each night, I prayed for somebody to come and rescue me.

Chapter 13

Not a Robbery

One morning, two weeks after Ivy had left, I woke to the high-pitched sound of the telephone ringing. In that same moment, my father burst through the front door and ran through the living room into the kitchen, a faint scent of his cologne floating in the air as he rushed to answer. Someone had called a couple of times earlier that morning, but I was too tired to deal with the ringing telephone. Now it seemed they were calling again. I pretended to be sleeping—the usual protocol when I wasn't sure if my father was drunk.

"I was in the shower, and Tina's sleeping," I heard him say to whoever was on the other end of the line.

Why was he lying? And where was he before he burst through that door?

He hung up the telephone, and his footsteps on the tile appeared to be moving closer to me on the couch, where I'd fallen asleep watching television the night before. Feeling his hand on my shoulder, I held my breath, bracing myself for unwelcomed advances. His touch repulsed me. As he shook me, I pretended not to notice.

"Wake up, Tina. Uncle Chester's dead," he said a matter-of-factly.

The words jolted me awake, instantly alert and bewildered. "What?" I uttered, my voice filled with disbelief.

"No one's sure yet what happened. It was a robbery."

Questions raced through my mind too quickly for me to speak. Everybody loved Uncle Chester. Who would do this?

"We have to go," my father declared, his tone devoid of emotion.

"Where are we going?" I asked, but he didn't answer.

I still had yesterday's clothes on. I jumped to my feet, headed to the bathroom to brush my teeth and wet my hair. He honked the horn. Grabbing my comb, I ran out the door to the car. Even though it was only eight o'clock in the morning, the sun was already blazing hot.

We sat in silence during the forty-minute drive to Aunt Colette's house. My father didn't turn on the radio or say a word, but was otherwise calm and his usual self. As we were driving, I found it strange that he wasn't upset that Uncle Chester had been murdered.

We finally arrived, and I raced up the driveway and through the front door, filled with the fear of what would come next, but knowing I had to face it, regardless. I made a beeline to the kitchen, where I found my cousins Sam and Tara sitting at the round glass table with Aunt Colette, all of them drinking coffee out of white mugs that had an ugly green stripe around them. Several other people were standing around. I proceeded to embrace her, but she sat motionless, her stillness making me think of the cold stone statues I had seen in front of important buildings.

The murmurs of conversation continued. "Didn't Chester fire Dub last week?" someone remarked. My father had gone back to work for my uncle after my parents' separated, but I didn't even know he was fired a week ago until now.

"I thought he did," said another.

"That might make someone like Dub awful pissed off," another person added.

I was old enough to know exactly what they were implying, but they spoke as if I wasn't in the room—or maybe they spoke that way exactly because I was in the room.

My father walked into the kitchen, and everyone fell silent. Aunt Colette's eyes locked on to him, the first movement she had made since I had walked in. She glared at him, not saying anything. Her look, and what everybody had said, had me wondering if he had killed Uncle Chester too. The idea left me nauseous. I backed away until I was up against the wall and made myself invisible by hiding behind the window curtain. The adults usually talked more freely if they couldn't see me. As the conversation resumed, I listened to them talk, piecing together what had happened.

"They say it was a robbery, but nothing was taken," said a guy I didn't know.

Somebody else said, "They made him get on his knees, put the gun in his mouth, and shot him."

After a few hours, my father drove me home. He left me at the house and embarked on another drunken spree. I sat alone with my suspicions for the next few days.

He returned on the day of Uncle Chester's funeral. He was drunker than I'd ever seen him and he reeked of alcohol and cigarettes. He ordered me to the car.

"Where are we going?"

"Colette's" was all he said.

I was relieved and excited until he put the old post-office jeep into first gear. I knew he shouldn't be driving in his condition. Holding onto the handle above the glove box, I prayed and kept watch. As he began to nod and sway, I shouted, and he jolted awake, sending the jeep swerving from one side of the road to the other before regaining control. My heart pounded with each near miss.

Finally, after what felt like an eternity, we arrived at Aunt

Colette's house. Somehow, we were still alive. As he turned off the engine, I let out a sigh of relief. I jumped out of the car and hurried to the front steps, eager to see my aunt—until I heard the song "He Stopped Loving Her Today" blasting through the stereo speakers playing inside the house. I waited for my father, who was several steps behind me, before opening the door and crossing the threshold.

Once inside, I could see Aunt Colette sitting on the sofa with a dozen beer cans in front of her on the coffee table. Her swollen face and bloodshot eyes revealed her anguish.

When she saw my father, Aunt Colette pulled herself up and stumbled and ran across the room to where we stood.

Her voice quivered with rage. "You," she said, shoving her index finger in my father's chest. "You killed my husband, didn't you?" She poked him again, harder this time, making him take a step back.

My father's face showed no expression. He grabbed her by the shoulders and effortlessly held her off. Then he released his hold, allowing her to unleash her anger upon him, as she beat his chest with her fists.

Sam must have heard the commotion—he came running from another room and pulled her away. Another man, escorted us out of the house. "Dub, you aren't welcome here anymore," he told my father sternly. The weight of his words crushed me—I realized that this meant that I too was no longer welcome.

A few days later, we were thrown out of Aunt Colette's rent house and stayed in motels for a week.

Chapter 14

Traveling Girl

As we checked out of our last motel stay, my father informed me that his eldest sister, Penny, had moved to Texas, and we would be visiting her. Although I didn't know her well—they'd lived in Illinois up until now and visited rarely—I had heard she was a hardass. She was known for treating Uncle Aaron like shit at holiday gatherings. Everyone would laugh and say they knew who wore the pants in the family. "Don't feel bad, Aaron," my father had once told him at a Christmas party a couple years back. "She treated us that way growing up too."

My aunt and uncle lived in Garland now, only ten minutes from Aunt Colette's. They had a three-bedroom red brick home with hardwood floors throughout. We walked into the house and into the kitchen, where Aunt Penny was busy frying meat covered in flour. Uncle Aaron sat at their kitchen table, which had six chairs. As we gathered around for dinner, my father's charisma turned on like a light switch.

With a mouth full of food and smacking loudly, he exclaimed, "Penny, this is the best home-cooked meal I've had in a while."

"Dub, stop smacking and talking with your mouth full," Penny said, annoyed.

"It's my false teeth, I can't help it." He laughed but nobody else did. Turning to me, he asked, "Isn't this the best chicken fried steak and mashed potatoes you've ever had, Tina?"

I smiled and nodded in agreement.

Aunt Penny, a tall, slender woman with short blonde hair, sneered. "Dub, what do you want?" she said impatiently. "Why are you really here?"

"We need somewhere to stay until I get on my feet, and Tina could use a woman's influence in her life. It's been tough on me without her mother," he said, his voice serious and sad. "And tough on her, too," he quickly added. I wanted to roll my eyes.

Uncle Aaron turned toward my aunt, and she nodded her head as she lit her cigarette.

"You can help me with my lawn business until you find something better," he offered.

"Thank you. It shouldn't take long to get back on my feet."

By the end of dinner, they'd had several drinks, and that was my cue to unpack and get settled. I ran outside and got my trash bag of clothes out of the jeep. I allowed my father to have the spare room with a bed, and I slept on a pallet in the other room that had a settee, coffee table, and marble statuettes. When he said I didn't have to sleep on the floor, that I could sleep in the bed with him, I simply said, "No thank you."

The next day, Aunt Penny took me to enroll me in sixth grade. As she drove us to the school, I sat in the car with my hands neatly folded in my lap, feeling grateful and relieved but also terrified—she was an imposing figure, and I'd already observed the way my father bowed in her presence. It was probably good if I did the same thing.

Aunt Penny's grandchildren and ex-daughter-in-law, Rhoda, were at the house when we got home. Mary was nine, and her brother Jerry was only five. I began seeing Mary every day after school, and we had the best time exploring the neighborhood on bikes and playing outside or board games.

One afternoon, Mary had to leave early. Everyone had already started drinking and the house was full of cigarette smoke, the television blaring with one of their usual shows. I wanted to get out of there. Rhoda and Aunt Penny were talking in the kitchen and saying their goodbyes.

As Mary walked out the front door, I followed her and announced, "I'm off to ride my bike." I was ready to feel the wind in my hair and the free feeling that being on my bike gave me.

My father, sitting on the sofa, declared, "Where do you think you're going? You

don't have permission to leave."

I stopped in my tracks and, with my hand on the screen door, and looking straight at Mary standing on the porch, said, "Why do you even care? You're hardly here, anyway."

Mary's eyes nearly popped out of her head. I froze. *Did I just say that out loud?*

His feet hit the floor, and he rushed toward me and struck my right cheek with his left palm. I stumbled to my right, falling onto the sofa from the force of the blow. Mary watched through the screen door, as she covered her mouth with her hands. He stood there contemplating what to do next, until Aunt Penny intervened, saying, "Dub, get your ass over here before I slap you."

He walked away, and I ran to my room, crying.

About five minutes later, Rhoda poked her head in my room and whispered, "Can I come in?" Our eyes met and I nodded yes, holding back the tears.

"I told them I had to go to the bathroom. Are you okay?"

She handed me a small piece of notebook paper. "Here's my number. If you ever need somewhere to stay, call me. I mean it, okay?"

I sat there staring at her phone number until I'd memorized it, but also wondering why she gave it to me. It was nice, but a little odd, since I'd only known them a couple of months. I fell asleep pondering all that had happened.

DESPITE THE ALTERCATION with my father, living there had been the best place since my mother died. I'd been attending school regularly, making straight As, and having sleepovers at Mary's house. Even though I was making good grades, it was impossible for me to make friends. I was the small, white-looking girl with a big rear end. The Black kids would make fun of me. The Mexican kids from the east-side-boys-gang would chase me home. The popular and smart kids in my honors classes rejected me too. I wasn't good enough for any group.

If the kids weren't pushing me into lockers, they were making fun of my clothes or body. My last-period teacher was not oblivious to this, and would let me out the back door five minutes early, enabling me to get a running head-start home.

Since I was having trouble making friends at school, I asked Aunt Penny if she'd sign me up for the basketball team that was through the Garland recreation league not affiliated with the school. If I could play, I'd have a better chance at making the team in seventh grade. And an added bonus would be that maybe I could meet some friends.

She signed me up and I joined the Yellowjackets team. I played forward and relished being in control of the ball. I enjoyed bringing it down the court, passing it to my teammates and watching them make a basket. Things were looking up. I even made a few friends. One girl lived a few blocks down the street from me, and we practiced on Saturdays and Sundays at her house. I loved everything about playing basketball—especially the feeling of winning. I was finally in my element. If I knew where Ivy was, I would have told her all about it. I thought that she would have been proud.

IN EARLY OCTOBER, my father left on a Friday night to go who knows where, and he missed work the following Monday. He was still working for my uncle's lawn business. I was worried my father was going to mess this up for us. I could feel the tension in the house growing, and I had this uneasy feeling that I wasn't exactly welcome. So, I spent all of Monday obsessing over what would come next. I couldn't imagine life without my best friend, Mary. On the first day he was missing, my aunt called hospitals, jails, and family members, looking for him. That evening, she told me he was out on a drinking binge.

If he wanted to stay out for a few more days, I thought, *I sure wouldn't miss him.*

A few nights later, I heard whispers at the kitchen table. I cracked open the bathroom door to hear their conversation. Uncle Aaron said, "We've already raised our kids, Penny. We made a deal —they could stay if Dub helped me with my lawn business."

"Well, the season's almost over. Stop bitching," she snapped back.

The next day at school, I spent the entire day worrying over what would come next. I just couldn't lose Mary. I needed her in my life. As I was running home, it finally came to me. I busted through the front door breathing heavy from the mile-long run.

Aunt Penny was at the kitchen table, smoking a cigarette and watching *The Dukes of Hazzard*. Uncle Aaron sat at the cluttered table as well, surrounded by scattered pieces of paper, and clicking his adding machine.

I calmed my breathing and walked over. "I have an idea. Could I help you mow lawns to make a little spending money?"

Uncle Aaron glanced over at Aunt Penny, raised his eyebrows, and said, "Well, that's a great idea," smiling big. Then he frowned. "The mower is self-propelled, but I'm not sure you're tall enough."

"I'm sure I can do it," I said, standing straight with my head high. "Give me a chance."

"I'll tell you what, I was paying your daddy ten dollars an hour.

How about I pay you five dollars an hour?" His grin grew exceptionally wide; he looked like he'd just won the lottery.

"That's awesome," I said, jumping around in circles. "When can I start?"

"I have two lawns I need to mow tonight, and I was about to leave. Let's go."

My routine following school was the same every day—I mowed lawns or practiced playing basketball, ate dinner, then slipped off to bathe and hide in my room for the night. I intended to work hard and stay invisible.

Four weeks later, my father burst through the front door as I was cleaning the kitchen table. I glanced at him as he stood in the foyer area.

"Get your stuff," he said. "Let's go."

When we arrived in front of my mother's house, my pulse quickened. I followed my father to the door. "It looks like the key still works," he said, proud of himself.

"Are we allowed to live here?"

"The key works, and who's going to stop me," he said, cocking his head to the side and shrugging his shoulders.

Someone had turned off the electricity, and we only had his lighter and the light from the lamppost shining in through the windows. But luckily, all the furniture was still in the house. I dropped my trash bag on the floor and plopped on the sofa and went right to sleep.

Now that it was just the two of us and he didn't have a babysitter, my father took me with him to the bars. Each was a small, dingy establishment, similar to Cookie's, where people wiped their feet on the way out. The thick air reeked of stale alcohol, sweat, and smoke thick enough to burn your lungs. In some of them, there was a jukebox shoved in a corner, and my father would give me quarters to pick out rock and roll hits from the seventies.

Afterwards, I'd skip to the bar and prop myself up on the stool next to him. I'd spin around until I was dizzy or bored, then whine that I was tired and hungry. My father was too drunk to notice the way the bartender frowned at him. He'd just keep drinking even after I climbed down from the stool and curled up in a corner booth.

When he was done, he would find me and shake me awake. He'd yell that it was time to leave as though it was my fault we were still there, and I was holding him up. Rubbing sleep from my eyes, I'd crawl from the booth and walk to the car half asleep. I'd bolt awake to the sound of the engine, praying we'd make it home safely and doing my best to keep him awake while he drove.

Once home, I made my way into the house, where I'd snuggle onto the couch for a few hours of rest before school. Sometimes, I'd skip school altogether, and spend the day sleeping.

Chapter 15

The Note

I was sitting on the couch one evening, staring at the television, when I heard a soft knock on the door. At first, it made me nervous, since I was alone as usual. I hadn't seen my father for several days. "Tina, are you in there?" a woman's voice said. "I can see the lights on. "It's Lena—open the door."

I was overjoyed when I realized that it was Pam's daughter. She had come looking for me. But why, and how did she know where to find me? We weren't even supposed to be living here.

My heart raced as I tiptoed to the front door. I hesitated when I got closer, worried how my father would react if he knew I let his estranged wife find out I was home alone. But my loneliness overrode my fear, and when I threw open the door, I launched myself into Lena's arms.

We sat together on the couch. Lena told me she came to visit with Aunt Colette, and I babbled about how I was looking forward to returning to school after Christmas break. I watched her expression change as she looked around. She was clearly concerned. "Where is everyone?" she asked, looking me in the eye. "Who's taking care of you? Do you even have running water or heat?"

I explained that for a while we were using an extension cord plugged into the neighbor's house, but that my father managed to get the electric turned back on even though the bank owned the house and the gas was turned off. But that I had an electric blanket that kept me warm at night, and that I also had two five-gallon buckets that I filled up every night from the neighbor's spicket, and it would be enough water to last me all day. Once I started talking, I couldn't help but tell her everything. "After Ivy left, my father started dragging me around with him, but he wanted to go to the strip clubs, and they stopped letting him bring me inside. So, he started leaving me home alone. I don't usually have enough food, so when I run out, I go next door and ask for something to eat. The lady lets me wash dishes for a meal. But when she doesn't have enough to share, I don't eat anything."

"You skip dinner? Like, this is a regular thing?"

"Yes." I looked away. "Most nights, when I go to bed, I feel pretty hungry."

Lena got up and walked toward the refrigerator. I followed her. She shook her head when she opened the door and found only half a box of baking soda and a jar of mayonnaise and a few slices of bologna and cheese.

"Please don't tell anyone," I begged. "I don't want to get in trouble."

She reluctantly agreed.

But when she turned to leave, I felt something break deep inside me. I knew I'd go crazy if I had to stay here alone even just one more day.

"Take me with you," I said. "Please, don't leave me here. I'll be good, I promise." I held my breath and waited for her to respond.

She stopped, looked around the house, and then at me before answering. "Okay," she said. "Grab a bag."

I let out my breath and ran for my room to pack. Before we left, I wrote a note for my father. That was the rule: if you're going anywhere, you leave a note. It said simply—*Moving to San Angelo to live with Pam and Lena. Love, Tina.*

As we drove away, I smiled for the first time in a long time, feeling as though the weight of the world had been lifted off my shoulders, at least for a little while. During the ride, I dreamed of the warm bed, hoping things in San Angelo would be different this time.

THINGS WERE DIFFERENT—FOR starters, they no longer lived in the country. Pam and Lena lived in a small two-bedroom apartment near San Angelo State University. I was still sleeping on a couch, but I didn't mind. It was warm, my belly was full, and I felt safe for the first time in months.

During my first few weeks with Pam and Lena, I tried to learn their schedules, so I would know how to best to stay out of the way. I also turned twelve. It was a lonely birthday, since Pam was at work and Lena was out with friends, but I was okay with that. The day after my birthday, I walked to the middle school and enrolled myself in sixth grade.

In the mornings, the three of us rose and left around the same time. We were all in school. Pam was in the university nursing program, and Lena was in high school. It felt good to have company and feel like part of a family.

But the nights were different. Lena would go out with her friends, and Pam was working. Lena let me tag along with her a few times, but she quickly tired of having a little sister around. I couldn't stand the thought of being home alone again, so I begged Pam to take me to work with her at the hospital.

"Pam, could I go to work with you?" I asked in my sweetest voice. "I really hate being alone here at the apartment. And I promise I'll stay out of the way, or I can help clean, or I can sit on the floor and keep myself busy."

"Well, I don't know, I might get in trouble." Pam hesitated for a moment then smiled. "But you know me, always ask for forgiveness instead of permission. Let's go, and bring something to keep you busy."

It turned out that I had plenty to do at her work. I'd play on the floor an hour or so and then Pam would let me wander the hallways of the psych ward. I'd walk around as if I was a nurse checking in on patients. I'd let Pam know if there was a problem, which minimized her back and forth trips down the hallways and helped keep her feet from hurting at the end of the night.

I had one patient that was my favorite. He was a comatose sixteen-year-old boy who'd been in a motorcycle accident. Pam said his parents should have let him die, but they were being selfish and wouldn't. I saw his mom in his room a couple of times and she cried a lot. It made me sad.

When I was in his room, I'd talk to him about television shows, tell him about my life, and sometimes, I'd try to get him to respond with his eyes or by moving his finger. I secretly prayed that he would wake up one day, but Pam said it would never happen. I always felt at peace when I sat with him and always wondered if, somehow, he knew I was there, and if he would ever wake up.

I'd been living with Pam and Lena for about a month when Pam began taking me to the bar at night. While she drank, I played poker with the old men, which made me thankful for those Sundays I learned to play poker at Aunt Colette and Uncle Chester's house.

I played good enough to win money and I'd stash it away because Pam always ran out of money at the end of the month. I think she spent more on drinking than she did on food. I watched her drink three-hundred-pound men under the table. It began to make sense to me, why my father was with her.

After hours of playing poker while watching her drink, I'd follow as she stumbled out the door and handed me the keys. I didn't think twice about driving since I'd driven her big Ford truck to feed the chickens two years before. But when we went to the bars, we'd take the Datsun, which had a stick shift. Pam had given me a quick explanation of how that worked. Most nights, I could cruise home in second or third gear, shifting as little as possible while praying I wouldn't get stuck at a red light.

One night, however, as I drove the Datsun home, I had to brake for a light. I popped the clutch when the light turned green and the car stalled. Pam yelled at me to get moving. The more I tried to get us going again, the more frantic I became. All I could think about was how much I hated that car. And how much I hated my life.

Three red light cycles later, a cop pulled up behind me and turned on his lights. I rolled down the window as he approached.

Pam leaned over me when the officer looked into the open window. "I've had too much to drink tonight and thought it would be best to let my daughter drive me home," she said, slurring her words.

He laughed, and then she laughed. I took in a deep, slow breath.

"How old are you, young lady?" he asked.

"Fourteen," Pam mumbled.

He must have accepted her answer, because he then explained how to take off without popping the clutch. "If you can get it, I'll let you go home, since you only have a few blocks left."

The cop stood to the side, watching me as his cruiser's red and blue lights bounced off of the surrounding buildings.

"If I go to jail tonight, I'm sending you home to Dub," Pam said as I put the car in gear.

Turns out, I work well under pressure. I stepped on the gas and let out the clutch as slowly as possible—it didn't stall. The cop followed me all the way home.

DURING ANOTHER NIGHT at the bar, not long after we got pulled over, I told Pam I was ready to go home. She wasn't.

"You little bitch—we'll leave when I'm goddamn ready to leave," she said in her loud, drunken voice. Everybody looked at me as the bar fell silent. I turned to leave. As I walked toward the door, Pam yelled out, "I have the keys and you're not going anywhere!" She was right—she had the keys—but I didn't care. I was done playing poker with old men to help her pay the bills. I had changed zip codes, but not much else. And I had less control of my life with her than when I lived at my mother's house alone.

It turned out I didn't have a new family, after all.

I walked to the nearest payphone. First, I dialed the Greyhound bus station and asked when the next bus would leave for Dallas. I had forty-five minutes to get there. Then I called for a cab. My last call was to my father. I knew he'd be at the store working—though he'd been fired, and he wasn't welcome in her home, Aunt Colette needed him and my cousin Sam to run the convenience store. I started talking as soon as I heard his voice.

"Daddy, I need to come home. Pam is at the bar and just called me a little bitch for the last time. I'm going to the Greyhound station and will be in downtown Dallas at eight in the morning. Be there to pick me up."

"How will you get to the bus station, and how will you pay for the ticket?"

I could tell he was already on his way to being drunk. My heart sank. But I didn't have any other options.

"I won a hundred and fifty dollars playing poker at the bar," I quickly explained. "I already called a cab. It's pulling up."

He laughed. "Okay, baby doll. I'll see you in the morning," he said before the line went dead.

Just then, the yellow cab driver pulled up next to the telephone booth and rolled his window down. "Did you call for a cab, young lady?"

"Yes. Yes, I did," I stammered as I opened the back door and slid onto the black vinyl seat. The driver looked in the rearview mirror and said, "You look awful young to be going to the bus station alone."

"Well, I just gave my father your license plate number. So, I better make it there. And I need you to stop at my apartment real quick so I can grab a bag." He shook his head in amused acknowledgement, but didn't say another word during the five-minute ride to the apartment and ten-minute ride to the Greyhound station.

Once at the bus station, I somehow knew what to do next. I walked to the ticket counter, stood tall, purchased a bus ticket, and a few minutes later, I was on my way back to Dallas. As we drove out of the parking lot, I had this feeling of excitement I'd never had before. It was similar to winning a poker game, but this feeling was even better. An hour later, I was fast asleep on the bus.

Chapter 16

Return to Dallas

As I stepped off the Greyhound bus, cold raindrops hit my face. I pulled my hoodie over my head and zipped it to my chin. I was unsteady on my feet following the ten-hour ride from San Angelo. People scattered in different directions, looking for their families. I also searched for my father's jeep, feeling both relief and panic. Part of me was relieved when I didn't see it, but the other part panicked as the reality of having nowhere else to go sank in.

I walked inside the front doors of the bus station to find warmth and a bathroom. My eyes scanned the room, and I couldn't help but see I was the only white person in the building. Determined, I located the bathroom, put my head down, hurried over into the stall, and took care of business.

Once done, I ventured back outside to look for my father again. Though the area had cleared, there was still no trace of him. I stood on the curb biting my fingernails and wondering what I should do, until I noticed a guy waving me over and calling my name. I recognized him as my cousin Sam's friend Rick, whom I'd met a few times at holiday gatherings.

"Hey," he said, smiling as I walked toward him. "Your daddy asked me to come get you."

"Okay." I didn't know what else to say since I barely knew him.

When I got in the car, he said, "You're twelve years old, right?"

"Yesss," I said, drawing out the word.

"And you swindled some old men out of money at a bar to buy a bus ticket to Dallas?"

"Mmhmm," I said, giggling.

"Wow, in that case, what can I expect you to do once you're seventeen, Tina?"

He started every sentence with an "R" like the dog Astro on the Jetsons.

"I don't know, conquer the world?" I said laughing hysterically.

Rick did most of the talking during the half-hour ride, entertaining me with jokes that made me laugh until the moment we pulled into the parking lot of the convenience store where my father worked.

I had assumed he was taking me to my house, the place I'd lived with my mother, and where Lena had found me.

"No, Rick. Take me home, please."

His gaze shifted away from me. "I think you should go in and talk to your daddy."

A sinking feeling filled my chest as disappointment set in. I stepped onto the pavement and took a deep breath before making my way inside. The familiar bell sounded as I opened the front door. As I rounded the corner, I saw my father busy preparing a bank deposit behind the cash register.

"Why did Rick bring me here?" I asked. "I want to go home."

"Your mother's house was sold by the court, and we'll be staying here for now," he stated as he continued to count the money.

"What do you mean, the court sold Mama's house?" I said, crossing my arms. "Why did you let them do that?"

"Brandy and the lawyers are handling it—they don't tell me anything."

I glanced down the aisle. The thought entered my head automatically: *That's where someone put a gun in Uncle Chester's mouth and executed him six months ago.* I looked back at my father, who stood there looking older than I'd ever seen him. His curly grey hair was thinning and combed to the front, and the five wrinkles going across his forehead seemed deeper. He'd grown a beard, and it was mostly grey. A pack of his Camel unfiltered cigarettes stuck out a little from his front pocket. His blue jeans looked worn.

"Go unpack," he said, pointing for me to leave. "Not much has changed, except it needs cleaning."

I choked back tears as I walked away—my father viewed crying as a sign of weakness, and he'd threatened to give me something to cry about if I cried. Losing my mother's house and the memories of my uncle's death consumed my thoughts, but I knew better than to waste my time asking him any more questions.

As I approached the door leading to the studio, the fluorescent lights flickered above me, and the sound of the pinball machines on the left grew louder. On the right, I caught sight of myself in a full-length mirror. I stopped for a moment, staring, wondering if I looked like her. I didn't think so. And everybody called me "little Colette."

Memories of my mother seemed distant and hazy, but living in her house had provided a comfort where I could cherish the good times we had together. I remembered us lying in bed, watching the *Carol Burnett Show* and giggling until we almost peed our pants. And the image of her making enchiladas while "Sweet Caroline" played on the radio was magical. In that moment, nothing else mattered but me and her. She would turn, throw her arms in the air and move her hips side to side, matching the rhythm of the song, belting out the lyrics. She would grab my hands, and I'd spring into motion as well, and we'd sing the chorus in harmony as we twirled.

A loud popping noise from the pinball machine jolted me back into action. Walking into the tiny hallway, I saw the bathroom and, with a few more steps, I landed inside the cramped shack. The makeshift kitchen had a sink perched on two cabinets, and a rotten egg smell coming from the drain. A small counter held a dish rack, a toaster, and a hot plate with an inch worth of dirt and grime on its surface. A grey loveseat that reeked of smoke sat opposite the portable shower wedged in the corner, which also served as a TV stand for the loft. The television's elevated position made it eye-level for anyone sleeping up there.

I threw my bag on the floor and climbed the ladder to the loft. At the top, I bumped my head on the low ceiling, distracted by the four-by-four foot one-way mirror to my right. Through the glass, I could see the entire store. On the window's ledge was an office intercom, an ashtray overflowing with cigarettes, and my father's Colt 45 revolver.

As I wondered where my father would sleep, I couldn't help but to remember Brandy's stern words to him: "You're not going to do to Tina what you did to me." The thought of sharing a bed with him sent a shiver down my spine. I decided right then and there to sleep on the couch downstairs instead.

Upon closing up shop that first evening, my father told me he was leaving. I knew that meant he was heading to the bar. Although I was relieved, he wouldn't be home with me, the idea of being alone in that place frightened me.

Before stepping out, he said, "I'm going to lock the main gate, and you'll be fine."

"Didn't the robbers cut the lock and kick in the door last time?" I mumbled, following him to the front door.

He tilted his head and shrugged. "Just point and shoot if anyone breaks in."

I watched him pull the chain-link gate closed and secure it to the pole with a metal chain and padlock. No one was getting in, and I wasn't getting out.

In the loft, I sat under the light of the television, keeping a watchful eye over the gun and praying my father wouldn't return before morning.

Every evening thereafter followed the same routine, except we stopped any attempts at having conversations. My uncle's store was located across the street from the West Dallas projects, and I could hear gunshots and sirens multiple times a night. It hadn't even been two years since my mother's death, and I was tired of my life. I contemplated putting the cold barrel in my mouth a few times, longing to be a normal twelve-year-old.

March had barely begun, yet my father had already decided that school was no longer necessary. To keep me busy, he had me monitoring customers through the glass, looking for potential shoplifters. If I saw anything suspicious, I was to use the crackling intercom to notify him.

Every day, I watched people come in and out, studying their interactions with each other, and with my father, until I grew bored or hungry. Occasionally, I'd beg him for a few quarters to play Donkey Kong or Galaga to help break up the monotony.

One night, I drifted off to sleep upstairs and awoke to the sound of Rick and my father's laughter. I could tell my father was drunk from his slurred words. A few minutes later, I heard footsteps on the ladder, causing my heart to beat faster. I turned toward the wall and pretended to be asleep.

But then my father's hand rested on my hip and my body tensed up. I prayed he'd pass out, but his palm drifted across my stomach, inching closer to my chest. That was my cue. I quickly crawled to the end of the bed and scurried down the ladder.

"Get your ass back up here!" he shouted.

Rick was sitting on the loveseat. His eyes widened, and jaw dropped with the surprise of my sudden descent. I shook my head no and sat on the cold tile floor.

"Tina Marie, you get your ass back up here, now!"

"Dub, leave her alone and just go to sleep," Rick intervened, his voice quivering with a mix of fear and concern. I saw my father struggling to get out of bed and climb downstairs.

Rick's gaze darted back and forth between me and my father. Finally, he jumped and moved to the bottom of the steps, holding his arms in the air. "Dub, you're going to fall. Just go to sleep." Rick's voice trembled as he spoke.

"Move out of my way!" And right then my heart skipped a beat as my father's foot slipped, and he nearly crashed to the floor. He caught himself.

"See, old man—go back upstairs and dream of the beautiful girls you ran off tonight."

"Fuck you," my father mumbled under his breath as he made his way up the ladder.

Rick grabbed a mat from the hallway and settled onto the floor.

The following morning, Rick was gone, but I felt lighter, and determined to fight back.

One thing was for certain: I had to stay on my toes. One night, I'd grab the gun, run to the bathroom, and stay in there until he passed out. Another night, I'd be sleeping on the sofa. And on other nights, I'd use the broom to shove the ladder against the shower, so he'd have to sleep downstairs. That only worked if he was plastered. But if he moved the ladder to climb into the loft, the noise would wake me, and I'd race back down it while he settled onto the mattress. I'd considered using the broom to push him off, right as he took one foot off the ladder to climb into bed, but I was afraid it wouldn't kill him.

My efforts to stay several steps ahead of my father were exhausting, and I knew I had to put an end to the charade.

One night, when he was getting ready to leave, he glanced up toward the loft to say goodbye. What my father saw was me pointing the gun at his chest.

"This is it," I said with a determination in my voice.

He narrowed his eyes and glared at me.

"I should just point and shoot if someone comes in and tries to touch me, right?"

"Yes."

"Okay, Daddy, I got it," I said in a childish tone, putting the gun back on the ledge. I stared straight into the television until I heard him walk out the door.

My plan appeared to work as the atmosphere in the studio shifted after that incident. From then on, I only discussed basic needs—food or money—with my father. Facing him filled me with confidence and sparked something deep within me, and I dared to think that, someday, maybe I could do great things. It was a thought I had never had about myself before, and I held on to it as tightly as I could.

Chapter 17

Do as I Say, Not as I Do

My father drove into a dimly lit parking lot with a big sign announced *MOTEL* in flickering neon red, casting a faint, eerie glow onto the cracked pavement below. Underneath, the word *ANCHOR*, in neon green, glowed inside an anchor. And in an instant, we no longer lived in the back of Miller's Drive-In—we had moved to Dallas's red-light district.

The motel room was big enough for two double beds, a round table with two chairs, and a dresser. There was a small fridge in the corner and a bathroom with a bathtub. I settled into my new home and took a hot bath, making me feel like a queen in her castle.

Every few days, either my father or Rick would drop by to give me money for food. There was a vending machine near the office that had a variety of stuff such as chips, soup, and ravioli. Sometimes, Rick would even surprise me with a burger and fries.

The Texas heat overwhelmed the old air conditioner in the room, and I had to use a box fan sometimes, but I didn't care—I was no longer a caged animal. I continued my routine of planning each day to help with the boredom and loneliness. Each night, I would read the *TV Guide* and circle everything I wanted to watch the next day. Then I would create a schedule of activities around my television shows that included when I'd eat, sleep, and exercise. I had more movie channels than before, and I watched whatever I pleased, from scary movies to cop shows.

For the most part, I was in heaven. Right before dusk, I'd make a quick trip to the vending machine, fearing that someone might discover a twelve-year-old girl living alone in a motel. I had seen way too many movies where girls were raped and killed. After the incident where I'd pointed the gun at my father, he kept it locked away in the jeep's glove box. This forced me to find other ways to protect myself. Pretending to be a boy seemed like the only option. I would disguise myself by wearing blue jeans, t-shirt, tennis shoes, and a baseball cap, and as I walked to the office area, I slumped over just a bit, putting my hands in my pocket, and walked in a "manly" style. If someone greeted me along the way, I simply nodded my head, as if to say, "what's up," with zero expression on my face. Practicing how to walk, talk, and act like a boy was also on my list of daily things to do.

One day, around noon, I heard a knock. When I saw Rick through the peephole, I quickly opened the door and threw myself into his arms. I craved his company—or any human interaction, for that matter. Then I noticed the two girls standing behind him. They both glared at Rick with their arms crossed as he and I reunited.

Rick introduced them to me. I thought Rachel was the prettiest—she had green eyes and long brown hair. Laura had blonde hair pulled back with a clip and blue eyes. Judging by their clothing —low-cut shirts, tight skirts, and very high heels—I figured they were strippers. They reminded me of the girls who danced on the stage at the bars my father took me to when I was younger. Suddenly, my thoughts were interrupted by Laura.

"Rick, she's not even a teenager. What is she, a charity case?" she asked while smacking her chewing gum and blowing bubbles.

"We're not going to babysit her," Rachel added.

Rick stepped inside the motel room and, turning to them, said, "Whoa. Hold your horses. She doesn't need a babysitter—she's like my little sister, who I check up on from time to time. And I thought you wanted a hot shower?"

The girls walked inside and sat at the round table near the door while Rick walked around and sized up the room. "You good here, Tina?" he asked.

"I'm fine. Daddy stopped by a few hours ago and gave me five dollars."

He turned again and opened the door, ready to leave. "Okay. We'll get out of your hair and find another place to shower," he said.

"No, wait, stay! Please. I have really good hot water," I insisted.

Laura looked at me and then at Rick. "I guess we can hang out with her for a while until work," she said.

Rick shrugged his shoulders, pulled a twenty-dollar bill out of his wallet, handed it to me, kissed me on the cheek, and left.

"You are so cute," the brunette said when the door closed behind him.

The other looked out the window. "Let's go lay by the pool," Laura exclaimed. They dug into their travel bags and pulled out bikinis. It was amazing how much stuff they had in their bags. Since I didn't have a swimsuit, I opted for shorts and a t-shirt.

We grabbed towels and headed for the pool, sitting in chairs side-by-side. I leaned back to enjoy the sun's heat on my skin. The girls began asking me questions, and soon, my life story was spilling out of me. I gazed at the pool as I shared with them my mother's death, the night Brandy left, and the long bus ride to Dallas.

"And that's how I ended up here," I said, turning to look at them. They were both sitting upright, wide-eyed, with their mouths open. Their surprise confused me. Wasn't everybody's life like mine?

After a brief silence, we leaned back into our loungers and gazed into the big Texas sky. They began to chat.

"We could get her a job," Laura said.

"She's not old enough," Rachel responded.

"Well, we can't leave her here all alone—she's going to get raped or killed or both."

Laura turned to me. "We can help you get out of this shithole and teach you how to take care of yourself like we do. We ran away at sixteen, and our boss helped us. It's been a few years, and we're doing pretty good."

I had no idea what they were proposing, but they seemed to care, and the thought of being independent sent a rush of excitement through me. "Let's do it!" I exclaimed.

We rushed back to the room and took turns showering. Rachel threw me a small scrap of fabric that turned out to be a dress. I slid the material over my twelve-year-old undeveloped body, pulling the neck up and the hem down. There wasn't enough fabric to cover my top *and* bottom.

Laura pulled out her make-up bag and patted the bed. Sitting next to her, I couldn't help but think about the days when I watched my mother put on makeup and false eyelashes. But I had never tried it. As Laura ran the small brush over my lashes, it clicked, and I understood what was happening.

"I'm a virgin," I blurted. "I don't want to be a prostitute like Molly."

Laura stopped suddenly, looked at me with raised eyebrows, and stared for a few seconds before speaking. "Who the hell is Molly?"

"Molly, you know, from that movie *Angel*," I said, pulling my head away from the eye-brush.

She laughed. "You don't have to have sex with anyone. Only pretend that you want to."

I sighed in relief and leaned back in to let her finish.

When we were ready, Rachel picked up her purse and pulled out a joint. "Ever smoked weed before?" she asked as she slipped it into her mouth.

"No, I haven't, but I've seen my sisters do it."

She smiled at me. "The men like it if you're relaxed." She sucked some of the smoke into her lungs and coughed as she passed the joint to me. I held it between my pointer finger and thumb just like she had, slid it between my lips, and inhaled deeply. My lungs felt like they were on fire. I started coughing and couldn't catch my breath, but I felt the effects of the weed almost immediately. I became relaxed. My usual fear and anxiety moved to the back of my mind, and excitement about my future independence took over.

Before I knew it, we were in a taxi heading for the club. Although it wasn't far away, it felt like we'd been riding for hours. The effects of the weed were already fading, and I no longer felt relaxed. Fear had crept down my spine and settled in my stomach. The voice in my head screamed for me to run, but I ignored it and pretended to be calm.

MY FIRST THOUGHT when we pulled up to the club and saw the sign that read "Girls, Girls" in red and white letters was that it reminded me of nights spent sleeping in my father's car.

As we walked toward the entrance, a secret hope arose within me that someone would intervene and prevent us from going inside. Unfortunately, nobody did. All I could hear was my inner voice questioning my decision. *Are you really going to do this?* It took everything in me to stand still at the bar as I nervously waited for the boss to come over.

The man towered over me by at least a foot, and his huge belly hung over his pants—pants that looked like they'd been slept in. He listened while the girls introduced me. "Are you serious? She isn't even close to eighteen," he said, laughing as he ran his hand through the greasy mop on his head.

"She's fifteen, but she desperately needs a job," Laura said. I stood frozen in fear, terrified that he would hire me.

He turned to me. "You can go up in a little while. Watch and learn." He turned back to Laura. "She looks scared. Loosen her up, or she'll never make it."

My stomach churned, and I fought back the bile rising in my throat. My inner voice screaming louder than ever, and I was sweating. Unable to bear the situation any longer, I mustered the courage to speak up. "I can't do this," I said bolting for the exit.

Laura chased after me and she stopped me near the door. No longer sister-like, she shook me, her nostrils flaring. "We spent a lot of time trying to help you, and we put our reputations on the line."

But it didn't matter. I couldn't stay. "I need to get out of here!" I yelled. People turned to look, and Laura released her grip. I ran into the pitch-black parking lot, gasping for air. Once outside, relief washed over me. The voice inside had calmed—I'd done the right thing.

Laura and Rachel followed me out, and luckily, the taxi hadn't left yet. We sat in silence during the ride back to the motel. Both of them were fuming, though I wasn't sure what upset them more—that their project had failed, or that they'd wasted their weed and cab money on me.

The moment the car stopped in the motel parking lot, I jumped out and ran for my room. Once again, Rick was there, waiting for me on the porch. He looked me up and down, taking in the slinky dress and makeup.

"Where the hell have you been? I was worried."

Tears streamed down my face as I told him about the day, from the pool to the strip club. I was sobbing by the time I finished. Rick stared at Laura and Rachel, who were standing quietly behind me. Now, their fear of Rick outweighed their anger.

"Go shower and get all that crap off your face," he said through gritted teeth.

As I let the hot water wash away the makeup, I thanked God for giving me the strength to leave that awful place.

When I came out of the bathroom, the girls were gone. Rick sat on the end of the bed and patted the space next to him. I sat down, but refused to look in his direction. I was ashamed.

"You never have to go to places like that." His gentle tone surprised me. "And you can always count on me if you need anything."

"If it's so bad, why do you go there?"

"Well, you see, I just . . . I mean, sometimes a man . . ." he trailed off. "Never mind," he said finally. "Just do as I say, not as I do."

The next day, my father showed up at the Anchor Motel and told me to get packed. "Pam and I are back together and we're moving to Red Oak."

"Why is Pam living there?"

"Her brother died, and she's living in his mobile home."

That made sense—she was probably squatting in his trailer. *Whatever*, I thought. Even though I felt less like a caged animal living in the motel room, the initial charm had long since worn off, after the incident with Rick's girls.

Chapter 18

Five-Finger Discount

My father took the exit off the interstate. We'd made the forty-five minute drive to Red Oak. I'd never seen stars with such clarity, but the sudden stench of cow manure made me gag, and I had to use my t-shirt to cover my nose and mouth so I could breathe.

The last time I smelled cow manure was in San Angelo. Memories of living with Pam and her daughter Lena came rushing back. The ding-dong I ate an hour ago wanted to come back up. I hadn't seen Pam since I left her at that bar. I wondered if she would still be bitter about me leaving, but more than that, was she really dumb enough to fall for my father's ruse, again?

My father pulled the jeep into a grassy driveway, nearly colliding with the white mobile home sitting in front of us. The headlights reflected off the flimsy structure, hurting my eyes until they went off.

The screen door flew open, bouncing off the other side of the mobile home. About the time the headlights went off, I saw the porch light flip on and Pam came waddling out and stood on the porch with her hand on her hip.

"It's about damn time, Dub. Where've you been?"

"I had to work with Aaron for a few days, and Tina wanted to come with me."

The hell I did, I thought to myself.

"Well, I guess every Tom, Dick, and Harry's gonna live here now," Pam said, throwing her hands up in the air and walking into the trailer.

I followed my father into the house, and he walked straight ahead into the kitchen, sat down at the table, and lit a cigarette.

I stood there with my black trash bag, waiting to be told where to go. "You'll have to sleep on the couch until we figure something out," Pam said, pointing to the living area on the left. The orange carpet looked filthy, and the brown couch was covered in black stains.

The next morning, I woke up early to the sun shining in my eyes through the mini blinds that someone apparently had left open. I ate a quick bowl of cereal and began cleaning the kitchen, hoping to ease the tension in the house.

Pam came strolling into the orange and brown kitchen looking for coffee, wearing the same pink nightgown she had in San Angelo and sporting the same pixie cut, but with jet black hair. Her face was pale and round, and she looked like a ghost—that was what she always said when she didn't have makeup on, and I was starting to see it now.

"You can use my niece's room at the end of the hall. Lena's room is on the right," Pam told me.

I wondered why I couldn't have used it the night before. Maybe Pam was punishing me for ditching her at the bar? "Okay, thank you," I said.

I passed my father coming into the kitchen as I went to grab my meager belongings from the den. He didn't acknowledge my existence.

Standing at the door of Pam's niece's bedroom, I saw a white-framed twin day bed on the left side of the room, with a white comforter that had Care Bears printed on it. The dresser was also white with random items on top that Pam's niece had left behind: brush, mirror, hair clips, photos, and jewelry. I packed them up along with the clothes that were still in the dresser and put everything on the shelf in the closet.

The following Monday, Lena dropped me off at Red Oak Junior High, and I walked through the front door to check myself into seventh grade. When the lady at the front desk asked for my transcripts, I told her I didn't have any paperwork from my last school, and she said, "That's okay, sweetie—we'll order them. What classes were you taking?" I'd learned that I could always enroll myself into the next grade level, even if I didn't finish the previous school year, because by the time they received my records, I was already making good enough grades to stay where I was.

I'd changed schools, but the bullies seemed to be everywhere, and Red Oak was no exception. Compared to the city kids, these bullies weren't that bad. They just called me names and made fun of my hair and clothes—nothing new. Every morning, I'd get up at six-thirty, catch the bus to school, and ride it back home. The ten-hour days were tiring, but it was better than being inside that trailer.

While waiting at the bus stop, I met Scott. He lived half a mile down my street. He had strawberry-blonde hair and sky-blue eyes and played football. We talked very little at first—I was painfully shy around him for some reason. He had beautiful, straight teeth, and I didn't want to talk too much, fearing he'd see the way my front teeth horribly overlapped.

One morning, a week or so into the school-bus taunting experience I was enjoying so very much, I was sitting a few seats in front of Scott, and he yelled, "That's enough! Leave her alone." All the kids on the bus, in unison, sang out, "Scott's got a girlfriend!" I didn't even look back at him, I kept my head down and just smiled.

On the way home that day, he sat next to me on the bus and

said, "They won't bother you anymore." I quickly glanced up at him, sure that I was turning red, and smiled—

with my lips closed, of course.

TWO WEEKS LATER, my father went to work on a Monday and didn't come back that evening. Pam was frantic. Over the next couple of days, she and I called his sisters, local hospitals, and jails —nothing, and not a word from him.

I was going through the motions because I knew he wasn't coming back anytime soon, but I had to keep her happy. After two days of searching for him, her worry turned to anger.

Pam walked into my room on the third morning and said, "Eventually, your daddy's got to come back for you. Until then, you need to earn your keep around here."

"Is there anything you want me to do?"

"For now, just keep everything clean like you have been," Pam said as she turned to walk out. Well, that wasn't so bad. I was worried maybe she was going to try and put me in a too-small dress and smear my face with lipstick, like Rick's girlfriends had. Or maybe put me behind a too-big mower, like my uncle did.

"And you'd better find a boy soon to get you pregnant," she yelled as she walked away down the hallway, "so you'll have someone to take care of you, because Dub's sorry ass ain't gonna do it."

Everyone had been saying Scott and I were together because we hung out and he taught me how to ride four wheelers and dirt bikes, but I still felt like a tomboy and wanted to do anything a boy could do. I thought of us as friends. Sure, we'd kissed a couple of times but that only happened because we played spin the bottle and truth or dare with Lena and her friends.

I wanted to keep Pam happy, so I cleaned the house and made myself invisible. Sometimes, I'd sit in my room daydreaming of what my life would be like if Mama was alive. Other times, I went exploring the neighborhood on the bicycle I had found resting against the side of the house. I would ride for hours, trying to come up with ideas of how to make money, but now that I was living in the country, none of my usual ideas were possible.

Not much had changed since San Angelo. Pam couldn't manage her money, and the last week of the month was always stressful when we ran out of food. One Friday morning, I was in my room, and I overheard Pam and Lena talking.

"Shit, there's no food in this refrigerator, and I don't get paid until Monday," Pam said, slamming the refrigerator door. Then I heard her open cabinets, and she slammed those too.

"I'm not used to having another mouth to feed," she said, while slamming the cupboard door.

"Mother, let's just go to the grocery store," Lena said.

"You're right," Pam said, as if Lena had suddenly stumbled onto a really brilliant plan. I felt like I was missing something.

Pam and Lena walked out the front door and returned an hour.

I walked into to the kitchen and saw Lena holding one grocery bag. They were talking about the drama currently ensuing on *All My Children* when I saw Lena take out a package of bologna, bean dip, and hot dogs from her purse.

"Were they out of grocery bags?" I asked.

"No, silly, we used our five-finger discount," Lena said, laughing.

I nodded as if I understood what she was saying. "Can I make a sandwich and have some chips and dip?"

"Of course," Lena said while locking eyes on her mother.

With a full stomach, I went for a walk to think it over. The constant tension in the house and hunger pangs were too much. I had to find a way to get food.

Desperate to make things easier, I asked Lena to teach me how to steal when I got back.

"It's easy as long as you have a little money to actually pay for a few things at the end," Lena said. "You grab a buggy, put your purse in the child seat, and begin shopping. When you get the chance, you stick a few items in your purse."

"But how can I help you? Like, if we go together."

"Oh." Lena thought for a second. "Well, I'll put items in the child seat, and you shove them in the purse while I'm still shopping."

"Okay, I'm ready," I said as I listened intently, taking it all in.

"When I was a kid, Mother taught me to make a scene at the cash register about how hungry I was, and I'd beg her to buy me a candy bar. She'd tell me we couldn't afford it and how poor we were and to put it back."

"Did it work?" I asked.

"The customer behind us almost always paid for the candy bar and would also slip me a ten-dollar bill sometimes," she said, laughing.

"I can do both things. When can we go?"

"I have some cash. We can go now, but don't tell Mother."

We tiptoed out the door, got into Lena's red Fiat Spider, and she drove us to Walmart. When we came home, despite saying not to tell her mother, Lena right away told Pam where we'd been and how I got a ten-dollar bill from an old man that was standing behind us in line.

"Well, isn't that something, Lena? Tina's a natural, and that will come in handy."

After that, I suggested to Pam that Lena and I go to the grocery store once a week, so we could stock up on food and not stress out at the end of the month. Pam agreed and that became our routine every Saturday morning.

I DESPISED living in the country in a flimsy mobile home that felt like we were sleeping outside when we ran out of propane, but I think I might have finally felt a twinge of happiness. I had a place—I was useful.

Lena and her friends smoked weed and drank. Before long, we were hosting parties. We'd play spades, crazy eights, or poker. I dominated all the card games, to the point, that everyone would fight to be my partner in spades. Once Lena, claiming me as her partner, yelled, "She's my sister and that's that!"

She'd never said that before, and I suddenly felt like I belonged.

A month later, Lena and her friends had started the night playing quarters. Scott and I had not been partaking in any of the extracurricular party favors—he was a Christian and went to church on Sundays. I guess you could say he was my best friend by now, and I was following his lead. The hazing was particularly intense that night. Lena was already tipsy and said, "You guys are like two bumps on a log."

There were about six other people there that night. I looked at him and smiled. He smiled back and said, "You want to try?" I smiled big, showing my teeth on accident, and said, "I will if you will." The whole table started yelling, "Shots, shots, shots!" We ended up taking two each. When we played spades that night, Scott proudly said, "Tina's my girlfriend and that's that, Lena."

I have a boyfriend? That was all I could think. I was stunned. Everyone was laughing, and I played it cool and laughed along with everyone. I was happier than I'd ever been in my life. But that only lasted a few weeks.

My father showed up the day after Christmas and told Pam some crazy story about why he'd disappeared. She believed him, and all was forgiven. My father found out about Scott, and he was not happy. The parties ended immediately too. I could now only see Scott on the bus riding to and from school. Scott and I were drifting apart, but oddly enough, I was fine with the change. I knew it would come eventually.

In late January, my father and Pam had a knock-down drag-out, as she would call it, and she kicked us out. As we walked out the door, she said, "Don't let the door hit you in the ass on your way out."

I had a good feeling I would never see her again, which was fine by me. I missed Scott a little, but I'd probably never see him again either, so there was no use dwelling on it.

Chapter 19

Run Away

When Uncle Aaron opened the door, he saw me first. My father always made sure I was the first person people would see when we'd show up to squat, knowing they wouldn't turn me away.

In a tired, hopeless voice, Uncle Aaron told me, "You know where your room is." Aunt Penny barely looked up as she pointed to the room down the hall. Neither of them said a word to my father. He just walked in like he owned the place and went straight for the kitchen to grab a beer. I went to my room to settle in and make a new plan.

I was determined to finish the seventh grade, especially since I'd never finished fourth, fifth, or sixth. To do that, I had to stay put. I just had to keep my head down, help mow lawns, and stay out of the way.

But eventually their patience thinned, and the tension in the air made me feel unwelcome. This time, I decided not to rely on my father to find me a new home. On the afternoon school let out for the summer, I went to Aunt Colette's house instead.

When she opened the door, I could tell she was happy to see me.

"Of course you can stay—you're my baby!"

Aunt Colette hugged me and kissed me several times like she did when I was little. For a couple of months, we had dinner together almost every night and watched movies in her big king-sized bed, but by the time I'd started eighth grade, she had begun dating a guy ten years her junior. She brought him home one night, and he never really left. I was jealous, and miserable that Aunt Colette wasn't spending her time with me. I stayed out of sight, hoping she would miss me, but she didn't.

When January rolled around and I turned fourteen, that old familiar feeling of being unloved and a burden on everyone around me had begun to creep in again. I was scared and lonely in that big glass house.

One day, I was walking down the hallway, headed to the kitchen when I suddenly stopped because I overheard Aunt Colette talking on the phone. "I don't know where Dub is, but I've already raised my children and I can't handle this," she said. I raced to my room, not wanting to believe what I'd just heard. I was crushed that the only person on this earth I thought loved me really didn't want me in her home anymore.

For hours, I sobbed and slept. After mulling it over all night, I decided she couldn't really have meant what she said. I came up with a plan: I would walk into her room and tell her I was thinking of running away. She would scoop me into her arms, proclaim how much she loved me, and would beg me not to go. "You can stay as long as you want," she would say as we cried together.

The next day, I walked into her room and into her bathroom and found her getting ready for the day. "Well, there's my Tina Marie," she said as if she was very happy to see me. My plan was going to work beautifully.

"Aunt Colette, I'm thinking of running away since Daddy hasn't come back for me."

"I think that's a good idea, maybe your daddy will wake up and straighten up for once."

"Yeah, maybe," I said, my head down as I walked out of the room, shattered by her response.

IF I WAS REALLY GOING to move out, I needed to find some work. At barely fourteen, I knew it was unlikely that I'd get hired for any regular job. Would anyone even rent an apartment to a fourteen-year-old? I briefly thought about going back to the strip club, but I swore I heard my mother in my head tell me she'd kill me if I did that.

A few days later, I asked Aunt Colette for advice, and she showed me how to change my date of birth on my birth certificate. I brought it to her and she made a copy of it first, then showed me how to white-out my year of birth and brought out the old type-writer to change my birth year to 1969. Next we photocopied that copy and just like that I went from being fourteen to sixteen.

The next day, I applied for work at a couple of fast-food restaurants. That night, I came home with a cashier's position at Church's Chicken. For two weeks, I went to school, ran straight home to change clothes, and then walked to Church's. At ten o'clock, when they closed, I'd catch a ride home with my manager.

I'd hoped that once I was working and making money, and could pay some rent, Aunt Colette would welcome me to stay. Instead, she was repulsed by my presence even more, because I smelled like chicken grease. She made me undress out on the porch and she'd immediately toss my clothes in the washer. After a couple of weeks, she started complaining that her washer smelled like chicken.

I couldn't take it anymore. That was when I remembered my cousin Rhoda's offer from a couple of years before and made the call. "Hey, Rhoda, it's Tina. Remember how you said to call you if I needed a place to stay? Well, I need a place now," I said.

To my surprise, and with no hesitation whatsoever, she simply said, "Absolutely. I'll be there in thirty minutes to pick you up."

Chapter 20

Summer School

When my cousin Rhoda pulled up in front of Aunt Colette's house in her new white four-door Corolla, I was waiting at the curb next to two brown paper sacks filled with my few belongings. I felt fragile, like a glass teetering on the counter's edge, but I was strong. And I was used to moving, of course, but this time it felt different.

I took one last glance at Aunt Colette's beautiful home, so central to my childhood dreams. As I stood on the curb, I could still picture Aunt Colette sitting hammered at the kitchen table, where she was when I shut the door quietly behind me. I thought about how I'd dreamed of living with Aunt Colette and Uncle Chester, having friends over for swim parties and fitting in with the cheerleaders and jocks, full of pride over my family's wealth and happiness. Over the last few weeks, I had convinced myself that I could actually play school basketball and maybe even earn a scholarship to college if I worked really hard. But those dreams weren't in the cards for me. Not living there, anyway.

Fifteen minutes later, we pulled into Rhoda's single-car driveway. The tan and brick house sat on a small lot; it paled in comparison to Aunt Colette's. It wasn't the first time I'd visited Rhoda's, I'd been to a couple of sleepovers before, but this time I'd be staying for a while—or at least I hoped so.

I collected my bags and followed Rhoda along a short walkway, past a black light post and manicured front yard, and into the living room. As I walked through the door, I was greeted by two pit bulls. They wagged their tails and nudged me with their snouts as if welcoming me to my new home.

Just then, Rhoda's daughter Mary came running down the hall. "We'll share my room," she said, grabbing my hand. "Come on." She was excited to have her older cousin come to stay, and that made me feel better about the whole thing. As she pulled me along, we passed her brother's room on the right, the bathroom, and Rhoda's room on the left, which was directly across the hall from hers.

With a new sense of hope, Mary and I listened to Air Supply and Journey while we organized her room for us to share.

I BUILT a routine at Rhoda's. I went to school in the morning, and when the afternoon bell rang, I rushed to Church's Chicken, where I worked the counter till ten o'clock closing. Then I headed home to fall into bed. I tried to make myself useful to Rhoda by cleaning the house, doing laundry, and babysitting Mary and Jerry, her kids, when I could. My grades slipped to average, but that was all I needed to pass. I was sleep-deprived due to such a tough routine, but I felt like I had an actual home.

Being in a stable home gave me the confidence to finally try out for the school basketball team. When I made the team, my dreams were finally coming true. Although my schedule got a lot tighter, it felt good to be part of something—to feel like I belonged.

I wished I knew how to reach Ivy to tell her about making the team.

All had been going well for a few weeks until the basketball coach caught me smoking cigarettes. "You got one more chance, Tina," she said. "If I catch you smoking again, you're off the team." I had been smoking for several months, but basketball was much more important. I quit smoking right then and there.

A month later, Coach called me to her office. I stood anxiously in front of her desk. It was never a good thing to be called to the office.

"Tina, I warned you," she said. "You're off the team."

"Wait, Coach, what are you talking about?" It didn't make sense. I could feel tears streaming down my face.

"Julie saw you smoking."

"That's not true coach—I swear to God!

But she didn't believe me. And just like that, I was off the team. Without playing eighth-grade basketball, there was no chance I'd make the high school team. That meant there was no possibility of a sports scholarship one day. An academic scholarship seemed impossible too, since I slept through most of my classes, exhausted from thirty-hour work weeks. Any glimmer of hope for a college education seemed gone.

ONE DAY, a girl sitting behind me in English asked me to pass a note to a girl in front. Soon, it became a regular thing. I was the in-between, and I was good at not getting caught.

Her name was Kelly and by the time she showed up in my life, I had again become the target of bullying. It seemed like every bully in eighth grade was gunning for me. Rhoda had started picking me up in front of the school because it had gotten so bad. But every-thing changed when Kelly invited me to sit with her at lunch.

I had waited until the bell rang after lunch period was over to go into the restroom. I'd rather be late to class than beat up. I heard someone else walk into the stall next to me. My heart started to race. I came out to wash my hands and there was Kelly, smiling real big.

"Hey, thanks for passing my notes."

"Yeah, sure—it's no problem at all."

"You never get caught. It's so crazy, how do you do that."

"I don't know, I guess I have a way of reading people," as I shrugged and smiled.

We were walking out of the bathroom and Kelly says, "why don't you come sit with me at lunch tomorrow, that fat girl won't ever mess with you again or I'll kick her ass." "In fact, I could teach you how to take her down, and once you fight her, no one will mess with you again," Kelly said, excited about the idea.

"Sure, I'll join you for lunch tomorrow and let me think about how to handle Terry. She really does just want to fight me." Kelly was getting ready to walk into her class and I said, "Hey, thank you, I really appreciate you helping me out."

"Of course. I'm looking for a new best friend, if you haven't heard," she said laughing.

I couldn't believe what had happened. Everyone knew not to mess with Kelly or her friends. This was going to change everything for me.

Kelly was the opposite of me. She was popular and pretty with her caramel-colored skin and big brown eyes. Her dark brown shoulder-length hair was cut and feathered like Kelly Garrett's from *Charlie's Angels*, and at a little over five feet, she was a couple of inches shorter than me.

We had been in honors classes together since sixth grade, even though I had moved in and out of the middle school several times. I had watched Kelly move effortlessly between different groups of kids. Everybody accepted her—the jocks, the cheerleaders, and the outcasts. Nobody messed with her, and she always seemed to get what she wanted from both kids and adults. I didn't understand how she held such power over people until we became friends.

Despite living with both parents, Kelly was mostly in charge of her own life. As Mexican immigrants, her parents spoke very little

English. Kelly was their lifeline to the outside world, and their dependence on her gave her leverage to do whatever she wanted.

Kelly and I had only known each other for a week when I talked my manager into hiring her, which meant even more time spent together for the both of us. Now, with the same schedules and no parental supervision, we partied and skipped school, always looking for the next thrill.

I was afraid of everything, and she was afraid of nothing. The first time we hitchhiked, it was scary.

Kelly wanted to have margaritas for lunch, but I wasn't too keen on drinking so early in the day. I thought surely the waiters wouldn't serve us since we were only fourteen, so I agreed and walked the mile to her house to meet her. When I saw that her mother's car was gone—our mode of transportation to the restaurant—I stepped inside the house and said, "When is your mom coming back?"

"I don't know. She should have been back by now. But we can get there on our own," she said, walking past me and out of the house.

As I followed her, I asked, "How are we going to get to there? It's at least five miles away and that's a long walk. And it's eighty-five degrees out."

"You always worry too much. Come on," she said, and she began walking faster. She lived a few blocks from a street with three lanes on each side, and once we made it there, she started walking faster, got a few feet ahead of me, and stuck her thumb out. "Fuck Kelly, what are you doing?" I yelled as I felt my face feel flush.

"I'm getting us a ride, silly."

"What. No, way!" In that same moment, an older man, in an old, white, four-door sedan, stopped. She opened the passenger door and started speaking Spanish to him. The next thing I knew, she had jumped inside, leaving me standing on the sidewalk.

"Get in," she blurted. My heart was about to pop out of my chest at this point and sweat trickled down my forehead

"How do we know this guy isn't going to kidnap us?" I whisper-shouted.

"We'll jump out at a red light if he starts going the wrong way," Kelly said, getting out of the car to explain her getaway plan. "But don't worry—he's my dad's age and even said we shouldn't be hitchhiking because it's dangerous, and he's going to take us all the way there. Now, hurry you're holding up traffic."

Not convinced by her logic, I reluctantly got in the back seat.

We made it to the restaurant safely, and when I got out of the car, my body felt like I'd ran a mile, but I also had a feeling of excitement I hadn't felt before, at least not that intensely, and I kind of liked it.

Every new adventure started just like that, with me attempting to say no and her giving me no choice but to do what she wanted. Over time, I began to enjoy the adrenaline rush I got when doing dangerous things with her. Whether it was hitchhiking, going to Six Flags, or dining and dashing, it felt like we were living on the edge and she had a way of getting men to pay for whatever we wanted.

I was having the time of my life, but it didn't take long before that life began to unravel. As the end of the school year approached, I'd already missed forty days. Despite all the fun I was having, I hadn't lost sight of my plans—I still intended to graduate high school and go to college.

A week before school ended, Kelly and I were summoned to the principal's office. When I asked if she knew what was happening, Kelly just shrugged. Walking down the breezeway, my stomach felt sick. I'd never met the principal before.

When we got to the main office, a woman pointed to the door with the little rectangle silver sign that read *Principal Sanchez*. Inside, a man stood behind a brown desk covered with stacks of paper. His hair looked greasy, but I knew it was just a hair-gel overdose I was seeing. A huge computer monitor took up most of the space on his right side, making him look even smaller than he actually was. Waving us in, he pointed to the two metal chairs with orange plastic seats that were so close to the door that he had to squeeze by to close it.

"You've missed more than forty days of school. You two will have to repeat the eighth grade," he said. "Of course, if you attended summer school, you could pass, but I'm not inclined to give you that option," he said sarcastically.

Kelly glared at him. I could feel the tension in the air between them.

Kelly grabbed my arm. "Let's go, Tina," she said, sounding angry.

We walked out of his office and out the school's front door.

I felt devastated. I turned to look at Kelly. "How can he do this?" I asked. "We're passing all our classes. I told you this would happen."

"Calm down," she said. "I'll figure something out. I always do, don't I?"

"You have to fix this," I said. "I can't fail."

Kelly looked stunned, her eyes wide. I'd never told her to do anything before.

We walked next door to the Tom Thumb grocery, sat behind the dumpster, and got high, and I tried to push it all out of my mind.

THE NEXT WEEKEND, Kelly called me over to her house. I figured I was there to smoke weed since her parents were out of town, but she had a plan.

"Principal Sanchez is on his way over," she said.

I started to pace. "What? Why?" I asked. I felt queasy.

"You're going to hide in the closet, and I'm going to seduce him."

My mouth dropped open as my mind reeled. I knew the plan had potential since men found her sexy and hard to resist. So, I let her shove me into the closet. I angled myself to have the best view of the living room sofa.

My hands shook as I waited. I held my breath when the doorbell rang and exhaled quietly when I heard a man's voice. I wondered if he could really be that dumb. Principal Sanchez's slim, short frame and slicked-down hair came into my view. Yuck.

"Why did you call me here?" he asked as he sat down on the blue suede sofa.

"You know why. Don't play dumb. I know you want me," Kelly said. "Just pass me and Tina, and I'll sleep with you right here, right now."

For a few seconds, he didn't move. Then he got up and walked to the kitchen and back down the hallway. He was searching the house. Kelly waited. I thought he might leave, but he sat back down as he considered her offer. Finally, he grinned. "Okay. You've got a deal." He grabbed the back of her neck and leaned in to kiss her.

"Okay, Tina. Come on out!" Kelly yelled. I watched Principal Sanchez's expression change as I slowly stepped out of the closet, afraid of what he might do. I had learned the hard way what a man could do when something he valued was in jeopardy.

He stood, his light brown face turning blood red. "Who would believe you degenerates?" he asked.

Kelly stood and smirked. "But what if they do?"

I stayed frozen, watching the standoff between them. Kelly stood tall, her chest puffed up. Principal Sanchez paced with his hand on his forehead.

"At the very least, there will be an investigation. What will you tell them when they ask why you came to my house on a Saturday?" Kelly asked.

His brow wrinkled. "I can't pass you unless you attend summer school," he said, his voice low. He sounded defeated.

Kelly smiled. "It looks like we're going to summer school, Tina."

Principal Sanchez looked at each of us, his black eyes flashing angrily before he turned and traipsed out of the house. When the door slammed behind him, I bent over with my hands on my thighs, heart racing, trying to catch my breath. "I can't believe you just did that."

Kelly was dancing around the house. "I told you I'd take care of it. I'll always take care of you." She laughed. "Let's smoke a joint before we have to go to work."

By the end of eighth grade, I told Rhoda I would live with Kelly for a while. That summer, my world fell off its axis.

Chapter 21

El Paso Vacation

It was after closing time at Church's that the real fun would start. Each night, Kelly and I would choose a different vice—smoking weed, drinking alcohol, flirting with boys, or stealing whatever we could get our hands on—anything for an adrenaline rush.

My routine was the same every day. I went to summer school for four hours a day, four days each week. No matter what, I didn't miss one day, even though it was a joke. The English they were teaching was the same thing I learned in my seventh-grade honors class. Same for the math—it was the seventh grade pre-algebra I'd already learned. After school, I worked. After work, I partied.

At closing time, the lock clicked on the front door of the store I'd turn on the boom box, and depending on my mood, Madonna or Led Zeppelin would blare through the speakers, while Kelly headed for the vodka stuffed in her locker. My manager pretended not to know we were drinking, since we were underage. But he had beer in his insulated coffee mug, and he'd be tipsy before we left for the evening.

When summer school ended in late July, Kelly and I decided to take two weeks off from work and drive to El Paso to see Ivy. She hadn't been back to Dallas since leaving three years before, and I missed her. I figured she and Kelly would hit it off right away, and I'd get to spend two weeks with my sister, and also prove to Kelly that I was Hispanic, since she didn't believe me.

Despite all our partying, Kelly and I managed to save enough money for a down payment on a brown old Ford station-wagon at a tote-the-note car lot, a high-interest, no-credit-check establishment. Kelly gave her mom the money and told her to sign the papers. The car was so run down that I was surprised it could make it down the street, but it did.

Preparing for the trip, Kelly filled up two ten-gallon gas cans and loaded them into the back of the car. She was terrified of running out of gas in the desert—but somehow not of breaking down in our dilapidated beater. We loaded our clothes and toiletries into the back seat and set out for our long trip.

But first, we made a pit stop at Kelly's uncle's house to buy some weed. A Hispanic man wearing a motorcycle jacket greeted us at the door. He welcomed us inside and then into the garage, where a dozen people were hanging out. It seemed all of them were drinking and smoking cigarettes and weed. It was loud and chaotic and I wanted to leave.

In the middle of the smoke-filled room sat a school desk with one of Kelly's uncles crammed into the tiny seat. As I stood waiting for the deal to be done, the desk-uncle took off his belt, wrapped it around his upper arm, bit down on the end, and started pulling to make it tight. I didn't know what was going on. Everybody was speaking Spanish, and I couldn't understand a word they were saying.

Suddenly, everybody focused their attention on the uncle in the middle of the room. They started cheering and shouting. I kept telling my feet to move, but they wouldn't. I couldn't be sure, but I had some notion of what was about to happen.

Another guy walked up to the desk with a needle in his hand.

He pushed the plunger a tiny bit and flicked the syringe with his finger like I'd seen on television. The group cheered louder before growing quiet. I felt nauseous like I might pass out. Time seemed to stand still.

A few minutes later, I heard the group cheering again. I must have blacked out, because Kelly was now seated at the desk where her uncle had been. The belt was around her arm.

"No, no, no, no!" I yelled as I ran to her. I couldn't let them do that to her. Kelly's eyes were wide as she watched me unfasten the belt. And she was quiet. It was the first time I'd seen her this way.

I didn't realize the crowd had stopped cheering until I stood and looked around the room. All eyes were on us, but nobody said a word. I was sure they were mad at me. "We don't have enough money to pay for the drugs," I said as I pulled Kelly to her feet.

They started chanting, "Kelly, Kelly. It's your time, niece. You need to do this."

"Listen, guys," I said, as I walked Kelly slowly toward the door. She was unsteady on her feet. "We don't know how this will affect her, and we have a two-week vacation ahead of us. Let's meet up in two weeks and we'll party all night long."

"Hey, she's alright. Let them go," her uncle said. "She's taking care of our niece and that's what she needs, someone who's got her back when we aren't around. But in two weeks, niece, it'll be your time—and no backing out then."

We took the gifted baggie of speed, ran out the door, and went on our way.

"What the fuck just happened in there?" I said from my seat behind the wheel. "What *was* that?"

"What do you mean?" Kelly asked. "We just got some free speed. Let's go," she added as she turned up the radio and started singing Madonna's "Holiday." As reckless as we were, I knew instinctively this was one rash decision too far. And I couldn't understand how at the time—she didn't."

I DANCED with excitement as I knocked on Ivy's front door. We'd been driving all night, tweaked out of our minds, and hadn't slept. When the door swung open, Ivy stood glaring at me. "What the hell are you doing here?" she asked.

I stopped moving and stared at her in disbelief. "Let us in. We're tired."

She opened the door all the way and stepped aside.

"You're high," she said, turning away and leaving us standing by the door. I followed her into the living room, Kelly at my heels, thinking that when she got the surprise out of her system, she'd be happy to see me. But the more she yelled, the angrier she got. "Why are you here?" she said as she stormed around the house. "It was stupid for you to come here; I have nowhere for you to stay." She was stomping around, picking up empty bottles of beer and old pizza from the night before, and throwing things.

Kelly and I went to the only empty sofa of three, the others were occupied by people who were sleeping so hard they didn't wake despite all the noise. The empty couch reeked of weed and stale beer. Ivy was right. We couldn't stay the night, let alone two weeks.

We climbed back into the station wagon, went for tacos, took another round of speed, and started the drive back to Dallas.

Chapter 22

Paddy Wagon

I got arrested for the first time just before my fifteenth birthday. Kelly and I were fresh off our El Paso road trip when she suggested we go to the grocery store.

"I'm broke," I said. Although I was still working, my paycheck was gone. My last dime had gone to buying the car and the trip to see Ivy.

"So? We'll use our five-finger discount."

Despite my stomach butterflies flapping their wings like crazy, I complied.

I thought about changing my mind as Kelly pulled into the Tom Thumb parking lot, but there was no turning back. The last thing I wanted was to disappoint Kelly. It wasn't like I had a problem with shoplifting, I'd been doing it for a couple of years. But I still felt uneasy, like my inner voice was trying to tell me not to go in there.

We walked side by side through the lot—Kelly confidently marching ahead, and me trailing a few steps behind. The closer we got to the entrance, the more I felt like I might be sick. Then I remembered I had the .38 special in my purse. I'd started carrying it after Kelly's cousin tried to rape me, which didn't end well for him. We put him in the hospital, but I came out of it with a broken nose. Next time, I wanted to be prepared.

I stopped and turned to her. "Maybe I should leave the gun in the car in case we get caught."

Kelly kept walking. "Oh, it'll be fine. You worry too much." She was right, of course—I did worry too much. And I wanted to be more like her.

Once inside the store, we separated. We had done this before. It was harder for security to watch us if we weren't together. While perusing the aisles for something to steal, I picked up a black eyeliner pencil and carried it with me, unsure if I would follow through. That's when I noticed the man in the gray suit. He looked like one of those undercover cops on *Cagney and Lacey*, and he was looking right at me. I knew I had to act fast. I moved to a grocery aisle, out of his sightline, threw the makeup behind some canned goods, and found Kelly. "Dump everything. We've been made," I whispered.

The man in the suit beat us to the front door, and he stood blocking the exit.

"Get out of our way," I said, trying to push past him.

He flashed his badge. "Let me see inside your purses first."

I began to sweat as Kelly handed her purse to him. He rummaged through it and then pushed it back into her hands. He pointed at mine. I opened my purse and held it out to him so he wouldn't look inside on his own. I knew if he felt the weight of it, he'd do a more thorough search. Seeing nothing, he grabbed Kelly's bag again, but the result was the same. He reached for mine a second time, determined to find something, and again I held it out to him. I knew he felt the gun when he grinned. My heart dropped when he pulled out the revolver.

"Well, well—look what we have here."

The man in the suit slapped the handcuffs onto my wrists so fast, like they did on television, except my hands were in front of me. Then he grabbed Kelly's arm, spun her around, and hand-cuffed her hands behind her back. We were clearly the major attraction at Tom Thumb that day.

When the paddy wagon door opened, Porcupine—affectionately nicknamed for his hair by those of us working at Church's—stepped out. All law enforcement came to the restaurant because they ate for free as a courtesy. He was one of my favorites. When I saw the disappointment in his eyes, I looked away. It hurt more than being caught.

After hearing the details, Porcupine walked Kelly and me out the door with one hand on each shoulder. He removed the hand-cuffs, put us in the backseat, and drove to the station without saying a word.

When the booking process was over, we were allowed to make a phone call. I called Rhoda, but it was Aunt Colette's son, Sam, who showed up. He didn't say anything, but I could feel his judgment. And just like Porcupine, disappointment seeped from him. I wondered if they thought I was wasting my life, that I was destined for better things.

Kelly ran out to greet me as we pulled up in front of her house. "Are you okay?" she asked, almost giddy. She didn't seem at all upset. I was furious. And ashamed. My life wasn't going the way I wanted it to, and I couldn't help but think that Kelly was partly responsible for that. I needed to get away from her somehow, but it seemed impossible. I knew she wouldn't just let me walk away.

The next day, Kelly's parents told me I had to leave. They also made her quit working at Church's, claiming, I was a bad influence. They made the decisions Kelly wouldn't, and the one I was too afraid to make.

I was relieved to be back at Rhoda's. With Kelly out of the picture, I thought I could get my life back on track. But it didn't take long to miss her—or maybe just the excitement she brought. I wanted to have fun, but I also wanted to go to college. All she wanted was to find a husband and have kids. And when I was with her, I couldn't say no to her, so being apart felt like the only choice.

I STARTED SPENDING MORE time with Louise, my twenty-something manager. Although it seemed she wanted to look out for me, she also liked to party with the younger crowd.

One Saturday night, I convinced Louise into going bowling. I was tired of the routine of hanging out at her house or going to the movies. We were heading to Fiesta Bowling Alley, she suddenly turned down a side street.

"Where are we going?"

"I want to get some speed for bowling," she said, glancing at me, her pale, freckled face aglow with excitement.

I was surprised. I had no idea she was into speed as it turned out. I had run away from it with Kelly. Now, here was Louise looking to score and I could barely manage my own life. So, I decided it didn't matter.

A few minutes later, she slowed to a snail's pace. "Wow," she said. "There's a lot of cars tonight."

"I'm going to wait in the car," I said as Louise pulled up to the curb. I wasn't familiar with this neighborhood, but I knew that it was one where I sure wouldn't be walking around alone at night. The area was not well lit, and it was filled with small single-family homes built in the 1960s, with one-car garages with broken down cars. A few of the houses had boats parked in the street and in driveways.

Something didn't seem right about the whole scene, and the butterflies in my gut started flying around again like they had in the parking lot of Tom Thumb.

"Oh, okay," Louise said. "I might be a minute, and it's cold. You gonna be okay?"

I thought about it. She was right; it was cold. But I really didn't want to go inside with her. Something was telling me I shouldn't. "Okay," I said finally, ignoring my intuition and getting out of the car. "I'll come with you."

"It shouldn't take too long."

I hoped she was right.

Louise knocked on the door of a small, rundown house painted in aqua blue and black. The front door had a crack running down the middle. When it swung open, a bug-eyed-guy stood there, bouncing nervously from one foot to the other, fidgeting and glancing up and down the street.

As much as I wanted to leave, I tried to follow Louise inside when she pushed past him. He blocked my way with his arm. "I don't know her. She can't come in here."

Louise rolled her eyes. "She's with me. It's cool."

He looked me over and gave me a look that I knew meant I shouldn't go inside, but I did anyway.

Once inside, the warning in my gut faded, but it felt more like a door slamming shut—so to speak.

I watched the guy walk down the hall before he took a right toward the back of the house. We stood by the front door, eyeing the people to the left of us sitting on the sofa. A moment later, Bug-Eyes returned with two small bags of speed. Louise handed one of them to me. I slipped it inside the cellophane on the back of my cigarette box, thinking it must be my reward for having to endure the detour.

As I turned and reached for the doorknob, I heard a male voice coming from the back of the house say, "Louise, aren't you going to come and say hi?" Louise started moving toward the voice. I grabbed her arm to stop her, but she pointed to the sofa and disappeared down the dark narrow hallway.

Six pairs of glassy eyes were staring at me. I acted like I belonged as I moved to the stained, grayish yellow couch and squeezed my small body into the only vacant space, trying to avoid eye contact.

This was a situation I knew how to handle. I'd gotten good at playing it cool.

"Anyone want to smoke?" I reached into my purse and pulled out a joint. There was nothing a joint couldn't make better when it came to this kind of crowd.

I was just settling into the worn sofa, and the high, when the front door landed on the floor with a loud crash. A large man dressed in black army fatigues ran over the door and into the living room. "Get down on the ground!" he yelled.

Convinced the guy was part of an elaborate ruse, I started giggling. Everybody else hit the floor. My eyes traveled from his face, down the length of the barrel of his shotgun, and into two black gaping holes. That's when reality set in. More men rushed in behind him and splintered off into different parts of the house.

"I said get down on the ground with your hands behind your head!" He was looking at me. I did as he said.

As I lay on the floor with the others, I thought about my purse with the baggie of speed in it. After getting arrested with Kelly, I couldn't afford for that to happen again; I'd end up in juvie for sure. I kept my eye on the man, and every time he looked away, I wiggled my toes in an attempt to push my purse under the sofa.

I couldn't have been on the floor for more than ten minutes when one of the men in fatigues dragged Bug-Eyes out from the back of the house. He stumbled into the living room with his hands tied behind him. The army guy who had been focused on me quickly turned and rammed the butt of his shotgun into Bug-Eye's jaw.

Get down on the ground," he ordered.

It was clear they were trying to rough him up on purpose, I knew right away—he was the nark

He turned his attention back to me. "Bitch, I told you to keep your head down. Give me one reason to blow you away. Come on, just give me a reason."

It was hard not to laugh, especially since my brain hadn't yet caught up to the situation. I was in the middle of a raid.

The SWAT team restrained each person with a zip tie before pulling us to our feet by the shoulders. Somebody shoved me toward the front door. I stumbled down the stairs and onto the lawn, right behind the drug dealer, who had blood running down his face.

The group of us were lined up like soldiers standing in formation on the first day of boot camp. When I heard girls whimpering, I thought about Louise and wondered where she was. I'd been so caught up in all the chaos, I had forgotten about her. I stretched my neck out to see the faces beside me. Louise was in line a few people away. "I'm so sorry," she mouthed when our eyes met. I just shook my head. With Kelly out of the picture, I thought my life would be better. I thought she was the problem.

One thing I learned from watching television was to keep my mouth shut. So that's what I did. When one of the officers held my purse up in front of the line, demanding to know whose it was, I stayed quiet. Although I knew he'd find my high school identification card, I stayed the course.

I trembled as he pulled out my bag of weed and my ID. With the weed in one hand and ID in the other, he headed right for me. Standing in front of me, the cop shoved the weed in my face.

"Where's the speed?"

I kept my mouth shut. I refused to meet his gaze, afraid that one glance into his eyes and I would meet the butt of his shotgun.

He smirked. "Don't worry, I'll find it," he said as he moved to the nearby car where he'd placed my purse. He then pulled each item out and laid it on the hood. I held my breath when I saw the cigarette box poking out of my purse. I started to pray.

I begged God to intervene as I watched the officer from thirty feet away. He opened the cigarette box, turned it over, and dumped the cigarettes out onto the car. Since the outside of the box was as white as the speed, it blended in, making it nearly invisible. I watched as the frustrated cop returned the contents to my purse, before ordering another officer to take me away.

After a while another officer grabbed me by the elbow and pulled me to where my purse still sat. He left me standing next to the car while he picked up the purse and dumped its contents, just as the other cop had. He was intent on finding speed. I kept praying. I needed God to let that little baggie stay invisible. If he found it, I was afraid I'd never be able to go to college or I might end up in jail like my sister Brandy, which was the last place I knew she'd been, and the last place I wanted to be. A drug deal had put her there.

When the second officer swept the contents of my purse off the trunk, and back where they belonged, I breathed a sigh of relief and thanked God for the assist. The officer shoved me into the back seat of the cruiser and slammed the door.

A few minutes later, the other door swung open, and someone shoved Louise into the car next to me. I turned to look out the window, away from her. We sat quietly until she whispered, "I'm sorry. Tell them you didn't know it was a drug house or why we were there. I'll take the blame." Tears slipped down her cheeks. I believed she was sorry, but that didn't change anything. Here I was again. I just shook my head.

Porcupine was at the station when we arrived. I could see him from the holding area where orange plastic chairs lined the wall. This time, he wouldn't even look me in the eye. Of all the people I didn't want to disappoint, he was at the top of the list. My heart sank when he walked away without saying a word.

I didn't move until an officer called my name from behind a desk. "Date of birth?" he asked. A smile spread across his face when I answered, and he started to whoop and holler. "Folks, we have ourselves a minor here!" He yelled as he tore the form he'd been filling out. The other officers began to yell along with him. I had no idea why me being underage was so exciting, but it didn't seem like the worst thing. Until another officer picked up my purse.

Instead of watching this time, I stared ahead at the wall in front of me and listened. "We only found marijuana on her." From the corner of my eye, I saw the officer set the cigarette box down. Three searches and no one had found the speed. God had come through for me, after all.

When the search was over, they sat me down next to a sobbing Louise. "They're talking an extra ten years just because you were in the house," she said through gasps. Her face was puffy, her red hair a frizzy mess. Mascara had run down her face.

"Calm down," I said. "Tell them we were on our way to go bowling and you stopped by to say hello to your friend. "You need to stick to the story, no matter what they say. Do you understand?"

She nodded.

A few minutes later, I was taken into a gray room that barely fit the metal desk and two chairs inside. It looked a lot like the interrogation rooms I'd seen on television. The waiting detective pointed to a chair, and I sat.

A second detective cut the white zip tie off of my wrists before moving to the doorway behind me. I sat on the chair's edge. The detective behind the desk pulled out a small recorder from the drawer and slammed it down in front of me. I'm sure he expected me to flinch, but I didn't. He hit the record button. "Tell us what happened."

I did as he said. "My friend Louise picked me up to go bowling. She told me she had to stop at a friend's house on the way."

"What happened when you went inside the house?"

"After walking in, Louise disappeared down the hallway. I was just sitting on the couch when the door burst open."

The corners of his eyes creased as he looked at me. "Is that really what happened?"

"Yes," I said. I told them the same story again. And again. They made me repeat it until finally they'd heard enough. When the seated detective became quiet, the officer behind me asked one last question. "Exactly what do you think you'll grow up to become, Tina?"

"Oh, that's easy," I said, pulling my shoulders back and turning to look him in the eye. "A police detective or FBI agent." They laughed all the way out the door.

Chapter 23

The Judge

They told me that my father was coming, even though I had asked that they call Rhoda. How did they even get his phone number, I thought? I wasn't thrilled—being reunited with my father in the form of a ride back to Rhoda's from the police station wasn't my first choice of how I wanted this day to end. By fourteen, I knew he was a bigger criminal than probably anyone else in the police station and I was in no mood for the most ridiculous satire of *Father Knows Best*. If there were any other driver offers on the table, I would've gladly accepted.

I wondered if he would be irritated by the inconvenience I caused. A part of me hoped he would be really angry—that picking me up from the police station would be like a lightbulb going off as to what a crappy father he'd been.

"Let's go," the officer said as he swung the heavy iron door open. "You're going home." I didn't know what home he was referring to, but it didn't matter. I was finally free from the windowless concrete closet I'd been locked in alone for hours.

I followed behind the uniformed man, his keys jingling on his belt, wondering what would come next. Before now, my brain was always on autopilot, constantly in survival mode, thinking and strategizing about my next move. But the fight was gone out of me. I was mentally and physically exhausted.

As we neared the front of the police station, I could see the profile of a man standing at the front desk, his dark brown curly hair wrapped around the bald top like a horseshoe. It was Sam; I'd recognize him anywhere. When he turned to face us, the chain from his wallet swung out and bumped against his faded blue jeans. Boy, was I happy to see his signature look!

"Are you Tina's guardian?" the cop asked.

"No, I'm her cousin. Her daddy sent me here to pick her up," Sam said.

"She's all yours—good luck with this one," the officer said, like he was glad to be rid of me.

Sam put his arm around my neck, nuzzled me into his chest, and knuckled my head the way he always did, his silver and turquoise rings sparkling under the fluorescent lights.

"Come on, Mina Tarie, I'm taking you home." I loved his nickname for me—my name all flipped around backwards—and was so grateful to hear it that I didn't question where he was taking me.

I breathed in the sweet, cool air of freedom when I stepped outside. It was nearly ten by the time I slid into the passenger seat of his white Buick Regal sitting out front.

"You look like you could use a cigarette," Sam said.

"I thought you'd never ask."

"I've only got Kools," he said as he popped one out of the soft pack.

"I'll take anything at this point." I would've smoked pine needles if it was all I could get my hands on. It felt so good to be out of the cell.

"I thought the police called Rhoda to come get me," I said.

"They did. Rhoda called and asked me to get you and take you to your father's."

"Wait, what? I can't go back to Rhoda's?" I asked, beginning to panic.

"Tina, we talked about it, and we think it would be good for you to go live with your father. He's married now. And he stopped drinking," he added, as though that would make me feel better about it.

"He's married now," I repeated numbly. There was no point in arguing; my options were limited.

"Yeah—to Nan," he said. "Remember her? I think you met her a while back at a family thing."

I didn't have the energy to respond and just nodded.

Ten minutes later, we pulled up in front of Nan's house, a small brick bungalow nearly hidden behind an enormous pecan tree. Two cars were crammed into a driveway barely big enough for one.

Sam didn't shut off the engine, so that was my cue. I took a deep breath and opened the door.

"This is for the best," he said as I stepped onto the sidewalk. I pushed the door closed without saying a word. I couldn't even look at him.

A yellow light flicked on as I walked along a short pathway to the front door. My father opened it a moment later.

"Hello, baby doll. Heard you got in trouble with the law. Just like your old man," he said and chuckled as a tall, barking Doberman came running up beside him. "Trixie, go lay down!" he yelled, moving to the side for me to enter.

As soon as I stepped inside, I was hit with cigarette smoke so thick and heavy it would rival that of any dive bar. The kitchen was just a few steps from the entrance. When I rounded the corner, I saw Nan, my father's new wife, standing near the doorway. She reminded me of an Amazon and was just as imposing. The big grey wig didn't help. I wondered what her real hair looked like under there.

"Are you hungry?" she asked. "Here, sit down," she said,

moving toward the kitchen table. Nearby, three of her kids were seated at a card table with dominos in front of them. Each of them held a cigarette.

"I wouldn't mind a Coke," I said as I sat in an empty chair. Although I'd met Nan and her kids a couple of years ago at Aunt Colette's, I still felt really awkward around her. I didn't even know she and my father had gotten together. Wouldn't Nan—like any mother would have, out of concern for her husband's missing kid —have asked my father, at some point, about my whereabouts? I wondered how that conversation might have looked.

"So, you going to tell us what happened?" my father said.

"Dub, can't this wait until tomorrow? I'm sure she's tired," said Nan.

I told them the same two-minute story I had told the police and asked if I could take a shower.

"Do you need something to sleep in?" my new stepsister, Kristy, who was four years older than me, asked. I was grateful for the offer since I had nothing but the clothes on my back. I nodded and followed her down a short hallway to her bedroom, where she found me some pajamas.

After I had taken a long, hot shower and put on the red and black flannel pjs, Nan showed me to the converted garage, now a game room, where she had made up the sofa sleeper for me.

"Get some sleep," she said. "It will be a busy day of cleaning tomorrow—every Sunday is." I had no idea what she meant, but my eyes closed before I could give it much thought.

The next day, it all came together. Nan was as much of a clean freak as she was a drinker. And it didn't take long for me to realize there was nothing new about my father. His wife drank just as much as him, and she cussed like a sailor. Turned out she'd been married to a man in the Navy, but he'd died a few years back.

Six days a week, they'd stumble out of bed and make their way to the small nearby liquor store where they worked, together—my father behind the cash register and Nan in the kitchen, cooking breakfast and lunch. After work, they'd go straight to the bar down the street to get plastered before coming home.

On the seventh day, they rested. Kind of. Sundays were for cleaning. The housework started early, earlier than any of us kids wanted to get out of bed. Since I slept in the game room, the room closest to the kitchen, I would awaken to Nan banging dishes around in the sink. I was sure she did it on purpose.

Then, predictably, she'd yell at my father: "No one ever helps me out around here!" She'd slam doors and ram the vacuum cleaner against the baseboards in an attempt to drive everyone out of bed. I don't know why she didn't just wake us. I wouldn't have argued. I would've done what I always did for a stable place to live —make myself useful and try to keep the peace.

My new step-siblings slept through most of their mother's rampages. They'd finally drag themselves out of bed later in the afternoon and do a few things to make peace with her. After dinner, I fell into bed exhausted, while the whole house would start to party. The steps liked to party as much as their mother and my father, and they did so almost every night while our parents were out. Nan gave them a weekly allowance, which they used for weed and whatever other drugs they could get their hands on.

It was a whole new experience for me. My father had always looked down on druggies; now, he was married to a woman who smoked weed and allowed her children to do the same. Nan didn't care how wasted any of us got as long as we stayed home to do it.

And it would start all over on Monday morning.

IN THE EARLY spring of my freshman year, my father sat beside me for my first court appearance. As we waited in the hallway on a dark brown wooden bench, a man wearing a tweed suit walked over and sat beside me.

"Tina?" he asked.

My father responded for me. "Yes," he said, although it sounded more like a question.

"I'm your daughter's lawyer. I need to speak with her alone," he said.

Without saying anything, my father got up and walked through the double doors of the courtroom.

"Soon we'll be standing before the judge, and he's going to ask you some questions. You just say yes. You'll be on probation for one year, and you have to stay out of trouble. Okay, let's go."

I could tell he just wanted to knock this out and get it over with, but I dug my heels in. "But . . . they shouldn't have searched me. They broke the law. Doesn't that matter?"

"No. It doesn't. You'll need to take the probation," he stated. "Now let's get in there."

As I followed him into the courtroom, where my father waited, I thought about all the questions I wanted to ask. Even at fifteen, I knew there was more to this than just agreeing I did what I was accused of. I wondered why we weren't fighting the fact that I should have never been searched in the first place. But he was the lawyer, after all. Surely, he knew better than me?

The seating in the courtroom looked like church pews without the kneelers. Parents and children were seated on both sides of the room, a wide aisle dividing it. When I looked down to the end of the aisle, I saw a white-haired man with a black robe, sitting elevated above everyone.

So this will be the guy calling the shots, I thought.

When the double doors swished closed behind me, I found my way to my father and sat beside him. A few minutes later, my name was called, I followed my lawyer, and stood before the judge. He asked me several questions, to which I responded as the lawyer had instructed me. And just like he said, I was sentenced to probation for a year. The conditions were that I check in weekly with a probation officer, pay a ten-dollar monthly fee, live with my father, maintain sobriety, and stay away from Kelly. As unreal as living with my father, his new wife, and her kids seemed, maybe that was where God wanted me to be? I decided to make the best of it. I didn't have a say in any of it anyway—even though this was my life.

The probation department was located inside the Garland police station. As I walked in, officers moved in every direction, buzzing with activity. I could feel sweat under my armpits and across my forehead, not sure if it was from my two mile walk or anxiety or both.

Outside the probation department, ten folding chairs lined the hallway, meant for people checking in and waiting to be called. At the front desk, I spoke to the receptionist, my voice quivering—I was more nervous than I had expected. She handed me a stack of papers to fill out, and as I waited to meet my probation officer for the first time, I fanned myself with them, trying to steady my nerves. I heard my name called and saw a short, round, black woman with gray hair around her temples standing in the doorway.

I followed her to her cubicle and sat in the chair that was up against the left side of her desk. "I'm Mrs. Cage, your probation officer," she said joyfully. I gave a quick smile, making sure, as always, not to show my teeth. I was also suddenly self-conscious of the bad dye-job in my hair. Kelly had wanted it blonde but instead it had come out a bright yellow.

"Well, you look like you've not had any home-cooked meals in a while. Your report says your daddy let you live with a friend for over a year?"

"Well, that's a lie. I ran away, and he never came looking for me, so I got a job at Church's Chicken and decided to make my own way," I popped back.

"I see you lost your mother when you were very young and your daddy hasn't done a very good job in raising you."

"Yes, that's right." Finally someone was seeing him for who he was.

"And he's the one that told you to smoke pot and carry a gun, too?"

"Ugh, no," I said, sheepishly.

"Good, we're on the same page—you've made some bad decisions."

"But you don't understand—"

She cut me off just as I was about to tell her everything.

"I don't know your exact story," she said, "but we all have a story, and we all have choices. I'm not saying it wasn't hard—losing your mom that young had to be devastating. And from the sound of it, you've been raising yourself for a while now."

I didn't say anything. I was trying to hold back my tears. I couldn't let her see me cry.

"I'm a mom," she said, "and I'm pretty sure this isn't what your mama wanted for your life. The choices you make over the next year—and for the rest of your life—will determine your future, not this one mistake." She paused for a moment and leaned in a little closer.

"You can still make your mama proud. Graduate high school, go to college, and the rest will come." Tears started to fill my eyes.

"Is it going to be hard? Yes. Even harder for you than most. But I believe you can do it. That's all for today. I'll see you next week."

I WOULD WALK to my check-ins every week—it was quicker than taking the bus. After three months, my probation officer pushed my weekly check-ins to once a month. Despite everything, I still dreamed of getting a college degree and making something of myself. I'd been praying more often since my drug-raid arrest, and trying to do everything right, but I still felt anxious all the time. I didn't know how I'd make it through the next year.

Every night, when I lay my head on my pillow, my heart would pound faster and faster. I didn't even know why. All I knew to do was pray. *God, if you get me out of this house alive, I promise I'll make something of myself.* I'd repeat the Lord's Prayer until I fell asleep and the recurring nightmare I'd started having would begin all over again: I would be walking out of our bedroom and my step-brother or sister would push me into the closet, where I would fall into an endless black hole. Needless to say, sleep was not always very refreshing.

While living at Nan's, I met Sophia, a tall, confident, twenty-year-old girl with salt and pepper hair hanging just past her shoulders. Sophia and Kristy had been best friends for a few years, but had grown apart after Sophia got pregnant, quit school, and married a marine.

Sophia had been over a couple of times, and we had lively conversations with great banter. Oddly enough, I worked at Church's Chicken and she worked at Kentucky Fried Chicken. We'd poke fun at each other about whose chicken was the best. That was until my father made me quit because of some weird phone call he received from the "labor board."

Sophia had been over several times and witnessed how Kristy and Joey teased me about everything—from my hair, clothes, and makeup to me being "smarter and better than everyone in the house." They resented me for choosing to live a clean and sober life and making good grades in school. I didn't get it. I was on probation and worked at a fried-chicken place—not exactly a stellar picture of perfection.

One Friday night, Sophia had come over to hang out, get high, and play cards. It turned out, she and I were unstoppable at spades. Tempers were flaring, and the teasing had started up again, and she'd had a little too much to drink. Sophia stood up, pointed her fingers at everyone and said, "Listen here, you sorry motherfucking losers, you're just jealous because she's actually going to make it out of this hellhole and you're gonna be here sucking your mama's tit until you're forty."

She grabbed her things and walked out the front door, motioning for me to follow. We sat out on the curb talking for a little while, so she could sober up. "Listen, Tina," she said, her tone serious, "the only way you're gonna survive a year with these assholes is to get a job and stay gone. I can get you a job with me if you want, but you gotta be damn good, because our store is number one in the district."

Of course I could be damn good—this was fried chicken we were talking about. "Sophia, I was a shift manager at fourteen at Church's. I promise I'm a hard worker."

"Alright, we'll see about that, missy," she said, ruffling my hair. Then she changed the subject. "Kristy's really changed in the last year. I haven't spent as much time with her since I got married and had my son—who you've *got* to meet real soon. But you gotta know, they're not gonna stop. You're gonna have to start fighting back. Figure out their weaknesses and make fun of them."

I laughed—though I really felt like sighing. "Okay," I told her. "Will do."

"I'll call you Monday about getting you a job. I'm tight with the manager, and you'll be working by next Friday."

Sophia kept her word and got me a job at Kentucky Fried Chicken. I threw myself into work, avoiding home as much as possible. On Sundays, I even volunteered for double shifts just to escape the chaos—it was glorious. For the next twelve months, I showed up to school nearly every day, clocked over thirty hours a week at work, and saved every dollar I could, counting down the days until I was finally free.

WHEN THE FOLLOWING MARCH ARRIVED, I made my last trip to see my probation officer, and she officially released me and told me not to give up on my dreams. We hugged goodbye.

On my walk home, I stopped by KFC, to tell everyone I was a free bird. Sophia had already spilled the beans. As soon as I walked in, they all started clapping, whooping, and hollering.

I wasn't home for more than five minutes when a huge fight

erupted between my father and Nan. I heard my name thrown around a few times, but I had no idea why they were arguing about me. Probably because "I thought I was better than them" or something equally stupid. I wasn't sticking around to find out.

I ran to my bedroom, stuffed all my belongings into two black trash bags, climbed out my window, and walked the mile back to Kentucky Fried Chicken.

My manager beamed when I walked through the door with the bags over my shoulder and said I had just "moved out."

"You did it?" he said. "You already left?"

A few co-workers gathered around to hear the story of my escape. One of them offered me her couch for the night. And just like that, my couch-surfing era began.

Chapter 24

Fresh Start

Sophia and I were on lunch break at KFC when she made an offer that changed the course of my life. "I've been talking to Terrance about your living situation, and we were thinking you could move into our extra room if you wanted to stay with us. Since your social security check is two hundred and fifty dollars a month, we would be fine with that as your monthly rent."

"That would be so amazing, but your house is in Rowlett and I don't have a car."

"Well, we've been looking at cars for you. You've got some money saved, right?"

"Yes, six hundred dollars."

"We found a nineteen seventy-one baby-blue Volkswagen Beetle for twelve hundred dollars. My mama said she could loan you the rest of the money."

"Really?" I said, with tears filling my eyes. I hugged her and thanked her profusely.

"Now stop that—people are going to think I've become a fucking softy."

I MOVED into Sophia and Terrance's home that summer and began falling in love with their two-year-old son, Bradford, who woke me up each morning with his sweet voice. "Tinie, time to wake up," he would say. On days that I was home, I spent a lot of time on the floor with him playing Tonka Trucks or listening to him tell me all kinds of stories—sometimes they made no sense, but I listened and smiled. He loved to talk, just like I did when I was a child. In between work and school duties, I showered him with as much attention as possible. I wanted him to feel important and loved.

As August arrived, I started my junior year at South Garland and walked inside not knowing what the future held. But I soon realized there were consequences for my previous actions. The teachers and administrative staff remembered me as a disruptive adolescent, and the fact that I had been bullied and tormented for years did not figure into their summary of my character. They saw me as I had been and not who I was trying to become. A simple change of heart on my part wasn't enough for me to succeed at South Garland—I needed to change schools altogether.

I needed a fresh start.

Since I had moved to Rowlett, I had the option to change high schools and attend Lakeview, but a simple transfer wasn't possible —I needed their approval first. My principal at South Garland told me that a meeting at Lakeview would be a waste of time, but I had to try.

On my way to Lakeview, I said a prayer, hoping God would come through for me again.

I walked through a glass door and saw five brown plastic chairs to the right of me, lined up against the wall made of glass, and a lady standing behind the attendance desk. She greeted me warmly and asked why I was there. She wore a cable-knit sweater that matched her purple glasses and a jar of peppermints on her desk. I told her my name and that I had an appointment with Vice Principal Green. "Oh, yes, honey, you're on his calendar. Have a seat in one of those chairs."

While we were waiting, she asked me why I wanted to transfer to Lakeview. I practically told her my life story in ten minutes. I started with my mother's death, and then about how I attempted to raise myself. Her eyes grew wider the more I talked. I continued by telling her how I'd been trying to better myself in the last couple of years, but I couldn't convince the teachers at South Garland I'd changed. Not to mention, the drive was thirty minutes and Lakeview was only fifteen minutes from my new home. A few minutes later, Mr. Green was ready for me.

"Good luck," the lady at the front whispered, leaning in like she meant it. I stood up and headed to meet my fate.

I walked into his tiny office that had enough room for a small desk and two wooden chairs. Behind him was a credenza covered with stacks of paper and framed photos of his wife and two boys. The walls were plain white with diplomas and plaques from awards he'd won through the school district.

The vice principal was a stern-looking man, fair complected, with wire-rimmed glasses, chubby cheeks and a full head of white hair. I guessed him to be in his fifties. With my palms sweating and my voice quivering, I started to tell my story.

"Mr. Green, I'm here because I just moved to Rowlett with a friend from work and I'm looking for a fresh start. I got into some trouble before, but I finished my probation and now I'm trying to get my education . . ."

He'd been staring straight into my eyes the entire time and when he interrupted me he said, "If you don't live with your parents, you can't attend any school in the Garland School District, let alone here."

I fought back tears. "Please, just give me a chance. I'm trying to do better. I promise I'll stay out of trouble."

Mr. Green stood, as if letting me know the meeting was over and prompting me to hurry along. "I will inform South Garland that you don't live with your parents," he smirked. I didn't budge. "I bet they'll be happy to know they no longer have to deal with you."

My resolve crumbled and, as the first tear slipped down my face, I stood, opened his door, and hurried out of his office.

"Tina, what happened?" the attendance lady asked as I burst out his door and through her little area, grabbing me by my arm.

I stopped, now in full-fledged hysterics, and tried to explain what happened. The words came out jumbled.

As she caught the gist, her back straightened. Her face became more and more red with each word I spoke. "Sit down," she said, pointing to the chair I'd only moments ago sat in, relaying my history with my heart bursting with hope. "Wait right here. Don't leave, you understand me?" Wiping my nose on my sleeve, I shook my head yes. She turned and stormed into Mr. Green's office, shutting the door firmly behind her.

I stared at Mr. Green's door, dark thoughts filling my head that I had. *I don't know why I keep trying. It's never going to be enough— if I drove off the Miller Road bridge, life wouldn't be so hard anymore. Maybe I need to stop fighting the inevitable.*

After a few minutes, the door swung open. The attendance lady locked eyes and grinned. "I got him to reconsider your attendance here. He has agreed, but on one condition," she said.

I sat up straight. "What? I'll do anything."

"You must report to me—only me—if you have any absences."

"That's it?"

"Yes. Now remember, I am responsible for you. Don't let me down." She wagged her finger at me as she spoke, but she was smiling.

"Thank you. I won't," I said, throwing myself into her arms.

Walking out of the building, every inch of my body felt at ease.

I IMMEDIATELY JOINED LIGHT BRIGADE, a support group for high school students trying to stay sober. We shared our struggles, gave each other advice, and somehow still managed to have fun. I didn't even know groups like this existed. Until then, I thought having fun meant drinking, or getting high—or both.

One night, some friends from the group took me to my first AA meeting, and it was similar to our Light Brigade meeting, but AA had an official program to help people stay clean. I didn't dare talk, and only listened to the stories that other people shared. Once the meeting finished, everyone stuck around, drinking coffee and tea, chatting like they'd known each other forever. A couple of random people came up and said, "We're going to IHOP if you want to join." Another group invited us to play games at someone's house. It was wild to see this group of people treat each other like family. I didn't know what to make of it, but I knew one thing—I wanted to know more about AA.

Transferring to Lakeview had proven to be a great decision. I had sober friends, and a stable home for eight months. That was, until Terrance and Sophia's partying escalated. Terrance had been clean for five years when Sophia told him she was unhappy in the marriage because he had become boring. In order to try and be the man she wanted him to be, Terrance broke his sobriety and started drinking, which lead to harder drugs in a matter of months. They partied until the wee hours of the morning several nights a week, making it difficult for me to get any sleep, and that started to affect my school attendance.

Close to the end of my junior year, they had become more and more reckless, and I worried what I might find each night that I walked into the house. I had to do something before it was too late.

One night, I came home around midnight and Sophia was sitting on the sofa alone, listening to music and playing solitaire. As I walked over to her, I saw several lines of cocaine on the glass table, next to a few crushed beer cans and an ashtray overflowing with cigarette butts.

"There she is!" Sophia greeted me from the sofa. "I wasn't sure if you still lived here. I never see you anymore—you're always off to your AA meetings."

"You're the one who told me to straighten up and do something with my life."

"That's because I knew from the first day we smoked a joint that you were different," she cooed. "But now you're so fucking boring and *don't want to have any fun!*" she added, yelling the last few words at the top of her lungs.

"Are the kids here?" I whispered.

"You know I don't do this shit around them."

"Why can't we have fun without drinking or using drugs?"

"Because I don't fucking want to, that's why," she smirked, lighting a cigarette.

"I'm worried about you and Terrance—maybe you guys should slow down for a while."

"I've got it under control, Tina. You worry too much. Go to bed," she said, glancing back down at the table and shooing me away with her hand.

I went to bed that night knowing I had to find a new place to live—on a budget of two hundred and fifty dollars. How was that even possible?

I thought about the times in my life when I had nowhere to turn, and somehow, out of the blue and totally unexpected would happen—and things worked out. Maybe this time would be the same.

Chapter 25

Denny's

I couldn't wait to take Mary to her first AA dance. In late July, my cousins Rhoda, Mary, and Jerry had moved back to Texas. They'd been living in Virginia for a few years, but Mary and I had picked up right where we left off. The one thing I missed more than anything about drinking was not being able to go dancing in nightclubs. AA sponsored dances—changed my life—and a sudden chance encounter set me on a course that I could have never imagined.

Mary and I had headed to Denny's to grab a bite to eat after a night of dancing. While we looked at our menus and chatted about what to order, I spotted two boys standing at the front door in the long line of people waiting for a table. The boys' eyes, which I could see looked bloodshot even from where we sat, flirted with us from across the room. Mary and I giggled as they begged to sit with us through silly gestures. One of the boys made his fingers do a little walking motion toward us, and then used his left hand as a plate and right as a fork, pretending to eat. Did they want to buy us dinner? Or more like breakfast, given the hour. We laughed and shook our heads no.

Not giving up, the other boy cocked his head to the side, puffed out his lips, pressed his hands together as if he was praying, and put one knee on the ground—begging us to come over. Mary and I looked at each other, laughing and trying to decide if we should let them eat with us. And next thing you know, they were walking toward us.

"You don't mind if we join you, right?" said the one with blonde hair and dreamy blue—albeit bloodshot—eyes, as he gently slid me over to squeeze into the booth. He was the one who'd begged on one knee, and now –somehow—he was actually sitting next to me.

"Well, do we have a choice?" I laughed.

He leaned in closer and softly said, "No, but we're buying your breakfast—and definitely getting your phone numbers."

The gentle bit of confidence caught me off guard, and my cheeks must have turned red. "We'll see about the phone numbers," I replied matching his playful, challenge.

"By the way, I'm Mason," said the blue-eyed boy." And this is Baxter."

While Mason and I exchanged flirtatious banter, Baxter had stood at the table, waiting for Mary's invitation. She slid over, looking at me with a smirk. "Guess we don't have a choice," she said, sarcastically. She may've been four years younger than me, and terribly shy, but she knew how to play the game.

The four of us spent a good hour talking while we ate. We learned they were sophomores at Garland High, listened to country music and rock-n-roll, and were part of an organization called the Masons. We gave them Mary's number, and they paid our tab, and we went home. We giggled over the chance encounter the entire drive home, excitedly analyzing which boy liked Mary and which boy like me.

THE FOLLOWING SATURDAY EVENING, Mary and I were getting ready to go out when the phone rang and Rhoda yelled, "Mary, it's for you or Tina!" Our eyes met, and we both crunched our eyebrows together, wondering who'd be calling. Mary picked up the phone. I watched as she was listening to someone talk and then told them to hang on. She put her hand over the receiver and whispered, "It's those guys from Denny's, inviting us to Mason's house for a party."

"Tell them we have plans," I told her.

She told him that, picked up a pen, started writing, and hung up. "Mason said we should stop by later," she shrugged.

Later that evening, we were driving back to Mary's house after going out, and I asked, "Do you want to drive by Mason's party?"

"Sure, why not?"

We pulled up slowly in front of his house and we saw the front door open, and through the glass storm door we could see inside the house and someone sitting on the sofa. From the looks of it, there was no party happening. Mason and Baxter came rushing outside. "Where is everybody? Is this the party?" I asked as we walked up the driveway.

"Well, it's close to midnight, and everyone has a curfew— except for the two of you."

We had some awkward small talk before I started walking toward my car. "Come on, Mary. We'd better go."

"Wait, when can we hang out?" Mason asked, following us, with Baxter right behind him.

I opened the driver's car door. "I don't know, I work a lot— actually, at that KFC around the corner—and I'm about to start my senior year. I guess call us," I said getting into the car. I looked into my rearview mirror, and they were just standing there, watching us drive away.

A FEW DAYS LATER, around closing time, I was standing at the front counter, closing out one of the registers. I heard the front door open and footsteps coming toward me. I looked up and jumped—it was Mason!

"Oh my goodness, you startled me. What are you doing here?"

"I'm hungry and came to get some food. Why else would I be here?" He flashed a grin, his eyes locking onto mine.

I nervously laughed, glancing behind me. The employees were in the kitchen snickering. "Alright, Mason—welcome to KFC—how can I help you?"

"I'd like a date with the manager. Her name is Tina," he deadpanned.

I busted out laughing. "I'm afraid to ask her, could you put in a good word for me?"

There are no managers by the name of "Tina" that work here, I popped back.

"Well, she looks like she's in charge even if she's not the manager."

"I think if you call her and ask her out, she'll probably say yes." I could hear the employees laughing behind me. "Please, you have to go now," I whispered, my face feeling flushed.

"Tina, I'm going to call you, but, just so you know, I'm taking you out this weekend," he said over his shoulder, walking out the door. I thought about that night after Denny's, when Mary and I were driving home. *I guess we know who he likes now,* I thought.

ON OUR FIRST DATE, we cruised Forest and Marsh in his dad's brand new Cutlass Supreme. Mason bragged about how the regulator had been removed, and he'd driven the car over one hundred twenty. We pulled into Taco Bell, hit the drive thru, and ate in the car while exchanging get to know you questions, avoiding the talk about my family as much as possible. We drove around, stopped to watch a few street races, and then headed back to Garland.

While driving on the interstate, I said, "So let's see what this car can really do."

He punched it and I watched the digital speedometer climb to one hundred, one ten, one twenty, before he let off the gas.

"Holy shit, that was awesome," I said. "Let's go again!"

After that night, many of our dates involved cruising around, listening to Guns N' Roses or Mötley Crüe and street racing. That's when I fell in love with driving fast cars.

The next weekend, Mary, Mason, Baxter, and I were watching a movie at Mason's house. Afterward, we went to grab food at the local Whataburger. We were struggling to come up with something to do that wasn't boring. As we ate, the boys asked us if we'd ever stolen pumpkins before.

In unison, we said, "Why would we steal pumpkins?" and they replied, also in unison, "Because it's fun—and way better than destroying someone's mailbox."

Next thing we knew, we were crammed into his mom's Ford Escort, stealing pumpkins off people's porches and setting them on a neighbor's porch a few houses down.

As the summer of 1988 came to an end, Mason and I spent more and more time together. I didn't think I'd see much of him once school started up, since I lived thirty minutes away and we went to different high schools. I'd seen this love story in countless movies. The guy and girl meet during the summer, have the time of their lives, then lose touch once school starts, drifting apart.

But that wasn't our story.

Chapter 26

Freedom

I started my senior year intent on graduating and ecstatic that I had been accepted into the *Distributive Education Clubs of America (DECA)* work program. This meant I would only have to attend four classes. But living thirty minutes away from work had become harder and harder. The only upside to working in west Garland was that Mason lived around the corner. And to my surprise, not only did he keep in touch, but he also wanted to be with me every chance I'd let him.

With a thirty-seven hour work week, going to school, and spending time with Mason, there wasn't enough time for much else. If I lived closer to work and Mason that might make my life easier and I could get more sleep.

Around Thanksgiving, I officially asked Mary if she wouldn't mind sharing her room with me again. I was nervous to ask Rhoda —I don't even know why—so Mary yelled downstairs, "Mom, Tina wants to move back in, okay?"

"Okay, but I thought she already lived here," Rhoda yelled back. We could hear her laughing. Jerry chimed in, shouting, "Me too!"

We laughed. Mary said, "I told you it was fine."

While I was closer to work, now I was far from school—most days, I was running late for class. I couldn't wait to be finished with high school and start my life.

In June of 1989, graduation day finally arrived. I had sent an invitation to my father simply to show him I didn't end up barefoot and pregnant, but for some odd reason, he wanted to go to my graduation.

Walking into the auditorium, I saw maybe a thousand people, none of whom I recognized, and I started to sweat. *What was I thinking? I don't see anyone I know.* I thought to myself. Michelle and I had DECA together, and I took her to work every day after school—I was hoping to see her at graduation. I hadn't thought my father would actually show up to my graduation, but I had warned her of his racist tendencies, just in case. She had responded, "He can kiss my Black ass if he does show up—he's not ruining *my* day."

Finally, I saw her, and she came running toward me. "We did it, Tina, we did it," she said, hugging me. "Hi, Mr. Cage, nice to meet you. I'm Michelle," she said, reaching out to shake his hand. He begrudgingly did so.

Mason said, "So you're the infamous Michelle that helps Tina push her Bug in the high school parking lot to get it started."

She laughed. "Yes, at least once a week, that damn car won't start—nice to meet you Mason—take care of my homegirl and fix her damn car." We giggled and ran to go find our seats.

Walking across the stage was anticlimactic. Instead of feeling wonderful and excited about the future, I had mixed feelings of anger and sadness. It hit me that this was only the first of many milestones I would celebrate without my mother. The drive home was quiet, and Mason and I had dinner with his parents to celebrate my graduation.

Now that I was eighteen, and had finished KFC's management training, and made more money, I could finally rent my own apartment. For the first time, life was finally in my full control—and it would go the way I wanted. Now I needed to figure out how Mason fit into my long-term plans.

As that summer came to an end, Mason talked more and more about him quitting school. We argued several times over it, but eventually I caved. I reasoned that school was harder for him because of his dyslexia, and while I wasn't dyslexic, I struggled with reading comprehension and, if I never had to read again, I would have been happy. We agreed he'd find a vocational profession instead.

Mason found a full-time job within a week of our discussion at a local oil change station and broke the news to his parents. They were not happy with his decision, but their marriage was on the rocks, and Mason said they didn't have time to fight with him because they were too busy fighting each other. He decided that he needed to figure out his own future.

By August, Mason began talking about moving into my apartment, but my heart felt like it was going to pop out of my chest each time he brought up the subject. I wanted to be independent. Up to that point, I'd had control over how much time he and I spent together, but he had become a tad clingy. I didn't want to complicate our relationship.

A few weeks later, he asked for a key to my apartment and I somehow dodged that bullet. That was until he found a clever way to convince me to give it to him.

One afternoon, I was working the mid shift when Mason stopped by KFC. "Let me have your key," he said. "I want to cook dinner for you."

"Really?" I asked, surprised. I handed him my key, with no hesitation, so excited that I wouldn't be eating KFC for dinner.

A few hours later, as I walked into the house, the familiar aroma of my favorite meal, beef stroganoff—Hamburger-Helper style—hit me instantly. But soon after, as I looked around, I started to feel as though the apartment walls were closing in on me. A television in the living room caught my eye—it hadn't been there when I left—along with a receiver, some speakers, a VCR, and a stack of movies. My eyes darted toward the bedroom. From where I stood in the kitchen, I could also see into the bedroom. My little black-and-white TV—it had been moved. My heart pounding, I stepped into my bedroom and froze—his boxes everywhere, invading my space. A wave of anger surged through me. "Mason, what have you done?" I said, throwing up my hands and buried my face in them. "We talked about this already!"

Standing at the bedroom door, he said, "Please, hear me out. I know you're scared to commit—and to say those three little words—even though I know you love me."

I sat on the queen-size waterbed with no fight left in me. He walked into the bedroom, sat next to me, and hugged me tightly and said, "I'm not going to leave you like everyone else—I'll take it all back home tomorrow if you really want me to."

He was right on all accounts. I was desperate for love, but too afraid to even think about that. Raising my head, my eyes met his. "I do love you, but know that if you ever hurt me, I'll hurt you in a way that'll make you wish you never had met me," I said, throwing my arms around his neck.

He laughed, hugging me tightly, and said, "Trust me, I know, I know. Do you want to take a hot bath before or after dinner?"

"I'm starving. After."

We watched MTV while eating dinner.

Before bed, I took a hot bath. He cleaned the kitchen and afterwards we spent that night unpacking boxes and making room in the dresser and closet for his clothes. I'd never told anyone, but I had been afraid of the dark since I was a little girl and, every night, I had trouble falling asleep. As unexpected as it all was, the idea of not being alone anymore was comforting. I slept like a baby that night for the first time in a long time.

Chapter 27

Family

M ason and I were doing our best to manage our new life and we had recently celebrated our one year anniversary. One night in mid-October, Ivy showed up on our doorstep. I must have stared at her for a full thirty seconds before throwing my arms around her and ushering her into our home. She laughed as she stepped inside. "Is that Mama's beloved marble coffee table?"

"Yes, Nan actually gave it to me, for graduation. She said it was ugly and that she never liked it, anyway."

Ivy got down on her knees and looked under the table and laughed. "Yep, the crayon marks are still there. That's the only time I remember Mama busting your ass for anything."

"You never told me about that," Mason said, as he took a peek at my four-year-old artwork that my behind had paid for dearly the day I created it. They were laughing as I grabbed my Marlboro lights box and said "Okay, okay—you guys have had your fun."

"I need a clean start, so I came home. Can I stay with y'all?" she asked somberly once we settled into the purple sofa with its ugly flowers—a cheap flea-market find.

"Yes!" I practically shouted.

"You have a sister?" Mason asked, overhearing the exchange from the kitchen. He was on hold with Pizza Hut.

"Oh, yeah—I guess I do," I said, laughing. At the excitement of seeing Ivy on my doorstep, I'd somehow skipped over providing him with that information.

Aside from knowing that my mother had died, and that I didn't talk to my father, Mason didn't know anything about my real family. I had told him that Rhoda, Mary, and Jerry were my "pseudo family" but never went beyond that. Having given up hope that Ivy and I might have a relationship after what had happened in El Paso, I just didn't mention her. It was easier that way.

But then she called me a few months back, and we had talked on the phone for a good hour, catching up on our lives and all that had happened in the very long time that we hadn't seen each other. I'd given her my address, because she was going to write to me and send pictures, but now here she was, sitting in my living room wanting back into my life.

"Ivy, I hope you like pepperoni and sausage?" Mason said, sitting on the floor with his legs crossed in front of me and Ivy.

"Yes, I'd eat anything right now—I've got the munchies—bad," she said, laughing. Mason, who was sitting next to me with his legs crossed, raised his eyebrows and

said, "You smoke pot?"

"Hell, yeah, and I'm gay too—hope that's okay with you." She said smirking, then added, "But if not, too bad."

"That's cool—we have something in common—I like girls and smoking pot too," he said, bouncing his body up and down as children do when unable to hold in their excitement. He did this often, which made his answer somehow even funnier. We erupted in laughter, and Ivy said, smiling, "Then we'll get along just fine."

And so it was decided. She would live with us in our five-hundred-square-foot apartment and sleep on the low-rider sofa until we could find a bigger place.

Ivy found a job soldering computer chips, and once we had three incomes, we rented a two-bedroom townhouse in Garland, which was only five minutes away from my new KFC store.

Things were good for a while, but Mason and Ivy both liked to smoke weed, way more than I did—I needed to be sharp at work. But that was only part of the problem in our new shared home. Two months into our new lease, tensions boiled over. Ivy and I had an argument—she wasn't pulling her weight around the house.

After a long day at work, I came home to a really dirty house. Walking through the front door, I was hit in the face with the smell of skunk weed and saw Ivy sitting in the living room in my favorite turquoise papasan chair watching *COPS*. I heard water running in the kitchen and dishes clanging together.

"What's going on?" I asked Ivy.

"I'm chillin' and Mason got home a few minutes ago and is cleaning the kitchen," she said, spitting her sunflower seed shells into her hand.

"I thought you were going to vacuum and pick up around here while I was at work?" I said irritated.

"I am in a little while. Stop nagging! You're always nagging us to clean, clean, clean," she said, in her bitchy tone.

I wasn't having it. "That's because you're a slob and do nothing to help out around here. All you do is sit around and get high," I yelled. She turned off the TV and stormed upstairs to her bedroom, muttering, "I don't have to take this shit."

We didn't speak the next day. Ivy moved to El Paso without warning, leaving Mason and me responsible for the rest of the lease. I had hoped we could finally be a family again, but it was clear I had only been a pitstop.

Chapter 28

Little Black Box

Mason and I made it through New Year's and celebrated my nineteenth birthday. A couple of weeks later, he popped the question—the one that most girls love to hear from their long-time beau.

It had been a long and chaotic week at work. I had been transferred to a store that had been performing poorly, which was my first assignment as an assistant manager. My job was to help the manager turn things around. That usually meant having to terminate employees, but my manager didn't have the backbone required to do that. Instead, she gave me all the shifts with the problem employees.

That evening, Tyrone, a high school football player, was not following kitchen protocol and appeared to be in no hurry to get anything done. Before the evening rush, I'd told him how much chicken and biscuits to cook. At seven-thirty, I discovered that Tyrone hadn't done as I asked. We were quite a bit short. When I asked him to quickly get more chicken from the freezer, he turned and walked away, moving at a turtle's pace and mumbling profane words about me and where I could go.

I walked around and stood in front of him. "Tyrone, you need to leave now—you're fired," I told him.

He puffed up his chest. "Make me leave, bitch!"

I didn't say a word. I simply stood my ground—all five feet, four inches, one hundred twenty-five pounds of me—staring him down and not moving an inch. I was almost wishing he'd hit me. I had some pent-up anger that I wouldn't have minded releasing in a scrap.

By then, all of the kitchen employees were at a standstill, and you could have heard a pin drop, but for the beeping fryers.

"Yo, man, she ain't worth going to jail over, is she?" one of the older cooks shouted.

Without taking his eyes off me, Tyrone ripped off his apron, threw it to the ground, turned around, and walked out.

"If anyone else here doesn't want to be a team player, you should leave now too!" I yelled—pointing to the front door.

Everyone immediately started working. It felt like my heart was trying to break free as I walked back to the freezer. But once inside the freezer, I buckled over as I tried to catch my breath and stop shaking. I took a couple of deep breaths, grabbed some chicken, put on my game face, and back out I went. I plopped the chicken on the table for the older cook, and he nodded and got right to it. I stood behind the front counter, I apologized to the customers and offered free drinks to everyone.

AN HOUR LATER, an employee came into my office to tell me Mason was there to see me. I sighed, putting my hands on my desk to push myself out of the chair, exhausted from the long day. When I stepped out, I could see him standing at the counter, his face lit up with a wide smile—beaming like a puppy whose owner had come home from work. As I stood behind the register, I leaned over and whispered, "Mason, this isn't a good time. I'm slammed."

"I really need to talk to you," he said urgently. "It's important."

I stormed out from behind the counter and into the lobby. He followed and met me by the door to the kitchen.

"Can't it wait?"

He shifted uneasily, rubbing his hands together. "No, it can't. I have something for you—but I'm afraid to give it to you."

I crossed my arms, bracing myself. "Mason, please. Out with it."

He reached into his pocket and pulled out a little black box, the kind every girl can easily guess the contents of.

For a moment, I was speechless, my first thought being that I wasn't ready for this. I was nineteen, and we hadn't been together that long, and there was school, the future I'd been planning and working toward. And a million other reasons why I wasn't ready. At the same time, I didn't want to hurt his feelings—knowing how deeply he cared for me. I was torn.

Smiling ear to ear, he opened the box, took out the ring, held out his hand, and asked for mine. When I gave it to him, he slipped the ring on my finger and wrapped his arms around me. He held me as though he were afraid to let me go. "I love you, baby, and I want to take care of you forever."

I said the obligatory "I love you too." He kissed me on the forehead.

"I'm never going to leave you. I promise," he said solemnly. "We're going to grow old together."

"It's beautiful. Thank you."

"Where's Tina?" I heard an employee ask. "I need help at the drive-thru!"

"I've got to go, Mason. We'll talk later." I turned and ran back behind the counter before he had a chance to speak.

As we were closing, what had happened started sinking into my head, and I wondered why he had proposed now—at KFC? Could he feel me pulling away? Our dreams and goals weren't the same. I didn't want children—I wasn't sure I even wanted to be married.

FOR THE NEXT FEW WEEKS, I tiptoed around any mention of the engagement. I wore the ring as I walked out the door, but the moment I got in the car, I slipped it off and tucked it into my purse. I needed space to clear my head. By then, Ivy and I had reconciled, so I flew to El Paso for a quick weekend trip and some moral support. Ivy's crash pad hadn't changed, but her five friends rushed to the door, eyeing me up and down. "We heard you needed to have some fun and figure out the rest of your life—let's have fun first," one girl said. Another approached me and said, "Have you ever been to a gay bar?"

"No, but I love to dance."

"Prepare to have the time of your life," she said. The whole group erupted, with someone shouting, "Hell yeah—let's go!"

I had the best time dancing—I hadn't done that in a while.

THE NEXT DAY AT DINNER, they peppered me with questions about Mason and why I hesitated to marry him. As we finished eating, each of them gave me their two cents on whether I should marry him or not. Ivy didn't say much of anything.

Driving to the airport, she finally said, "He loves you, but do you love him?"

"Yes. I mean, I think so."

"You came here wanting me to tell you that you should marry him. If you love him, marry him."

Ivy's words swirled around in my head as I stared out the window into the bright white clouds for the one-hour flight back home. Walking off the plane, I made a decision. I couldn't wait to tell Mason that I was all in—and there he was, waiting at the gate, holding a red rose. I ran to him, kissed him, and hugged him tightly. I'd definitely made the right choice, but now was not the time to tell him—best to keep us both on our toes.

Chapter 29

Someone's Going to Jail

Shortly after I returned to Dallas, I ran into my step-brother, Joey, while pumping gas after my day shift ended. It was a surprise—he lived across town, not to mention I hadn't seen or talked to Joey since I crawled out of my bedroom window at his mom's house years ago.

"Hey, Tina, crazy seeing you here. Mason's party last weekend was something."

I shrugged. "He knows how to have fun. That's one of the things I love about him." It didn't matter to me that Mason had a boys' night out with his friends.

Joey grinned. That's when I noticed he was more fidgety and awkward than usual.

"I hate to be the one to tell you this, but I'm pretty sure Mason slept with Tonya while you were gone."

What? I did a double take. Who was Tonya?

"How did you even hear about the party?"

"I went with Tonya, I didn't even know it was your house until I got there."

"What a weird coincidence that I haven't seen or heard from

176

you in years and you find out about a party—at my house—while I'm out of town."

"Yeah, weird," he said walking to his car.

My heart sank as I got into mine. I didn't trust Joey one bit, but I needed to know the truth. I drove as fast as I could to Baxter's house. If anybody could confirm the truth, it would be him—he was a horrible liar, and I could easily read him.

The moment Baxter cracked the door, his stubbly face looking tired and a bit confused to see me there, I asked, "Did Mason have a party while I was gone?"

He opened the door wider. "Well, come on in, Tina."

"Did he, Baxter? Tell me the truth," I asked, storming past him into the foyer. I stood behind him with my arms crossed and waited for him to turn and face me.

Baxter moved his weight from one foot to the other as he turned toward me. "Yes," he said finally. "Who told you?"

"Did he sleep with Tonya?" I asked, trying to control my emotions. I knew I was raising my voice and getting in his face, but I had little control at that point.

"I think so," he admitted. "But Mason was plastered."

"How does that make a difference?" I shot back.

"Look, I don't even know how Tonya heard about the party—people just started showing up. Next thing you know, she was begging him to do shots until he couldn't see straight—which was odd since she'd come to the party with another guy. I'm not even sure Mason remembers," he added.

"I appreciate you telling me," I said, walking out the door. I was surprised he told me all that he did—why did he? Maybe the story was true? Either way, Baxter had done his part, and I raced home to confront Mason.

When I pushed through the townhouse door, it slammed off the wall behind it and almost popped back and hit me. Mason jumped up off the couch.

"Did you sleep with her?" I asked.

"What are you talking about?"

"Tonya. Did you sleep with her, Mason? It's a simple question."

"No, I didn't sleep with her. Stop acting crazy."

"Yeah, well, I just came from Baxter's, and he said you did."

Mason's eyebrows raised and his mouth fell open. He began to walk toward me saying, "I'm sorry, Tina. I swear I don't remember what happened. Baxter told me the next day, right before I came to the airport, what he thought had happened. I don't even know how she heard about the party. It was only supposed to be a few people, and the next thing I knew, thirty people were here. I'm sorry. Please forgive me."

Forgiveness was the last thing from my mind. I was enraged. After everything I'd been through, his cheating was the last thing I needed. I started screaming at him, took off my ring, and threw it at him. I grabbed items off the kitchen counter and started throwing them. His keys, the saltshaker, the pepper shaker whatever I could get my hands on. He was dodging the items as he ran toward me like a soldier running through a field of landmines. He grabbed me by both shoulders, and I flailed like a fish. He finally pushed me against the wall, held me there, and begged me to calm down.

I broke down crying.

It didn't seem like we had been fighting that long, but then there was a knock at the door and Mason let me go.

"What the hell do you want?" I shouted as I swung it open.

When I saw the two Garland police officers standing before me, one with his hand on his gun, I froze.

"We got a call about a disturbance," one of them said.

"We're fine," I said. "Just having a disagreement. We'll quiet down," I said, closing the door. One of the officers put his hand on the door to stop me.

"That's not going to happen. Someone's going to jail tonight, and you better start talking or it'll be you." They separated us. I told one officer what happened, and Mason told the other. Twenty minutes later, they took Mason away in handcuffs. He was charged with assault, because even though he was just trying to calm me down, he had held me up against the wall.

That night, I stayed alone in the townhouse. Instead of sleeping, I lay awake until four in the morning, listening to the building creak and groan.

Mason went to his parents' house when he was released from jail the next day. I felt heartbroken. Neither of us called the other. His father came by the townhouse to gather some of his clothes.

A few days later, he called and begged me to take him back—I told him that I was moving into a new apartment with a roommate and moving on with my life and he should come get the rest of his stuff.

He didn't have my new phone number so he had resorted to calling me at KFC. If I had my employees tell him I wasn't available, he'd show up at the end of my shift, hoping for a conversation.

I couldn't trust him anymore. Instead of giving into him, I spent my time partying with old friends. At first, it was fun to let loose after being in a serious relationship for so long. But at night, when I went home, I was alone again in the dark, unable to sleep. Mason was all I could think about. I wondered if the crazy story Baxter had told me about Tonya was true—it seemed too crazy to be real. And I missed the way Mason drew my bath, managed household chores all the little things I had not noticed until he was gone. I'd always taken care of myself, but Mason—he just wanted to make my life easier. At least that was what he had said before.

A month later, on a Thursday night, I was tossing and turning in my bed, my mind racing. I thought about everything I was giving up by cutting Mason out of my life. That was when I reached for the phone. We talked for hours that night, about all that had happened, and everything we wanted for ourselves and each other. He told me he loved me more than he had even loved

Regina, his first girlfriend, which I had been secretly jealous of even though I didn't know her.

Before we ended the call, I invited him over to talk and see my new apartment.

The next night, when the doorbell rang, I rushed to open it. There he was, standing before me, his sky blue eyes locked onto mine. He stepped forward and I let myself melt into his embrace—he was wearing my favorite cologne. In that moment, I knew, deep down, that letting him back into my life was the right decision.

He followed me into the living room, where we sat together on the couch. When I reached for a Marlboro Light, he reached for his lighter. I smiled. "I miss you," I said, taking a drag. "I really want to make this work."

"I love you, and I'll do whatever you ask to earn your trust back."

I leaned into his chest. "It will take time for me to forgive you."

"Why don't we go somewhere, just me and you. Let's go to Padre," he said.

"Oh my God, that's a great idea." We had never been away together, and an eight-hour drive would give us plenty of time to reconnect.

A couple hours later, when it was time for Mason to leave, we stood in the living room and hugged goodbye. After pulling away, he reached into his pocket and got down on one knee. He gently grabbed my hand and slipped the ring back onto my finger.

As he was about to leave, I said, "What about your mom, is she really mad at me?"

"Don't worry about her, I'll talk to her, and she'll be fine."

I looked at the ring and smiled as he walked out the door. We were going to be good—I was sure that he was the real deal.

Chapter 30

Goodbye

I couldn't wait to see Mason. It had been a few days since he had been to my new apartment—I had been working the night shift a lot. He had been sick with seasonal allergies, so we hadn't talked much in a few days. From the KFC drive-thru window, I could see an older couple in the parking lot holding hands and walking to their car. They reminded me of how I wanted us to be. It had been too long, and I needed to see him, especially at this time of the year, just a couple of days before the anniversary of my mother's death.

Seeing Mason was all I could think about. That night, I was getting off at eight, and we had planned to go out, but since he still wasn't feeling good, he asked me to go to his house instead.

He seemed somber. He really didn't feel good. Earlier in the week, he'd told me he'd had a really bad headache for a couple of days, nothing like he'd ever had before. The doctor said it was a bad case of a sinus infection. We cuddled on the couch and watched a movie.

As I was leaving his house, he told me he planned to talk to his mom the next day, and tell her that we were getting married. He asked me to come over after work, so the three of us could clear the air. "You and mom are the two most important people to me in this world, and we will fix this."

"I'll do whatever she needs me to—for us to all be okay again."

WHEN I HADN'T HEARD from him that afternoon, I decided to call to see how the talk went with his mom.

When she answered, her words were short and to the point. "Mason's sick and can't talk to you right now." I could tell she still resented me. I knew that he still hadn't told his mom what had really caused the fight that landed him in jail.

"Mom! Give me the phone," Mason said in the background, his voice sounding weak. I heard him say something else, but he was mumbling. When I started to respond, she hung up.

I called again an hour later. I had barely gotten out my name when she said, "Mason's very sick and we might take him to the hospital." And again the line went dead.

After getting off work, I went home and sat chain-smoking by the telephone. I couldn't imagine why he'd need to go to the hospital over allergies. At just seventeen, he was healthy and strong, and didn't have any medical issues that I knew of.

I didn't realize I'd fallen asleep until the ringing telephone woke me. I checked the clock before picking up—I'd been out for over an hour.

"Mason is at Baylor Hospital." It was his sister Cassie.

"I'm on my way."

"I'm not sure Mom will let you see him, but I thought you deserved to know," she

said. "He would want you to know."

"I'm coming anyway."

The sun was beginning to set when I left my house. At the first stop light, I admired the pink, purple, and orange sky. *He would want you to know.* What did Cassie mean by that? Was he not able to speak? The blaring sound of a car horn snapped me out of my head—the light was green.

When I got to the hospital, I raced to the front desk. "My fiancé, Mason," I said, panting. "They just brought him in."

The nurse frowned at me and pointed to chairs behind me. "I'm sorry. His mother said you aren't allowed to go back."

I didn't respond, and there was nothing I could say. I stumbled to a chair sobbing, and just sat there waiting. I begged God to intervene. I couldn't explain it, but something in me knew this wasn't going to end well. I had told my roommate the night before, through tears and full-blown hysteria, "He's going to die," and she said I was overreacting. But I couldn't stop crying. *Please God. You can't do this. Please don't take him too.*

Finally, over an hour after I arrived, a nurse came out and sat next to me. "Why don't you go home, honey. Call in the morning, and we'll tell you how he's doing."

"I just want to see him and tell him I love him. Isn't there anything you can do to get me back there?" I sniffled.

She hugged me. "I wish I could. It's best you just go home and get some rest."

I did as she said and cried myself to sleep while begging God not to take him. The next morning, I abruptly woke out of a deep sleep. I wiped my eyes as I glanced at the red numbers on the digital clock—it was just after ten. A few minutes later, I was on the phone with the hospital. When the operator put me on hold, I lit a cigarette.

As soon as I heard a woman's voice on the line, I started talking. "This is Tina. I'm calling to get an update on Mason." There was only silence. I could hear her breathing, but no words came. My heart started to pound in my ears.

"Hello?" I said, my voice cracking, panic rising in my throat.

Then, almost like a whisper traveling through static, I heard her say, "I'm so sorry. He expired eight minutes ago."

Expired? The word didn't register. I sat on my bed frozen with my mouth open and unable to form a single word.

The red colon on the clock blinked. The world stood still.

I didn't move until the piercing dial tone screamed through the receiver, ripping my heart in two, fueling the rage that consumed me.

I slammed the phone into its cradle so hard I nearly tipped over the nightstand. Tomorrow would mark the ninth anniversary of my mother's death. This had to be some sick joke, I thought. My eyes locked onto the clock, and I pulled its plug from the wall socket and threw it across the room. I took each of the trinkets lining the headboard and threw each one at the wall, until I grew tired, fell on my bed, and began to sob. There was nothing I could do. He was gone, and I didn't even get the chance to say goodbye.

I made my way to the kitchen and grabbed the bottle of vodka from the counter. Then I drank. Flashes of anger interrupted a sadness that felt like it might kill me. My brain couldn't make sense of it—just two nights ago, we were planning our wedding. I raged at God. "How could You do this?" I asked the empty room.

Cassie visited a few days later. We sat together on the couch while she answered the questions I didn't have a chance to ask while Mason was in the hospital.

"He had bacterial meningitis. The doctors said he might have survived if he'd gotten to the hospital sooner."

"If he'd been with me, this wouldn't have happened," I said.

She reached over and put her hand on mine. "They also found an inoperable brain aneurysm. Mason wasn't slated long for this earth." We sat together in silence for the rest of her visit.

Half an hour later, when she rose to leave, Cassie turned to me, her jaw tight and her fists clenched in frustration. "It wasn't right that my mom wouldn't let you see him before he died, her voice filled with anger. But you know how stubborn she can be."

At the door, Cassie paused, her eyes brimming with tears. She leaned in for a hug. "I know you two had your issues, she whispered, but Mason always told me how much he loved you."

"I hope that means something." she added, her voice filled with emotion.

I pulled back, feeling the weight of her words, but I couldn't shake the ache in my chest. "I don't know if it does," I whispered my heart heavy with the unanswered questions."

Suddenly, the tears came flooding. I collapsed onto the couch, sobbing uncontrollably until the exhaustion overtook me and I fell asleep.

Later that day, I answered a call from Mason's mother. I hadn't heard her voice since that day she hung up on me with Mason's voice in the background asking for the phone. Now, her voice was softer, but just as short. She was inviting me to Mason's "celebration of life."

"This is Judy," she said, although I knew her voice well. "You're a part of this family, and you should be here." The celebration had already begun.

It was dark by the time I got to their house. The garage, where the food and drinks were set up, was lit and open. Chairs were scattered across the driveway and lawn, with some people sitting while others mingled. Guns & Roses heavy riffs and Clint Black's heartfelt country ballads blared through the neighborhood as some mourners played cards and dominoes.

My first stop was the bar for a beer. I didn't want to feel anything, but not even a case of beer would have been enough. I spent the rest of the night talking with Cassie and Mason's friends, trying to keep my mind busy.

At nine o'clock, Mason's parents went to bed, and an hour later, Cassie and I began the cleanup. When we were done, it was time for me to leave. Part of me didn't want to go—I knew walking out that door meant leaving the last part of him behind. But the truth was, I had no say in it. I'd never really had a choice about my life. And now, at 19, it felt like that would never change.

IN THE DAYS TO COME, when I was alone at night, I'd rage at God and cry myself to sleep. There hadn't been any contact from Mason's family until a couple of weeks later, when Judy, Mason's mother contacted me. She invited me to go shopping at Sam's Club with her and Mason's father. I was surprised to hear from her, but she had always taken me and Mason with her before he died. It was odd and random, but she was grieving. I wondered if she felt guilty because she didn't let me say goodbye to Mason, or if she missed having a child at home. Either way, it felt nice to be wanted. I accepted the invitation, and they bought me enough staples to last me six months. Before long, they were doting on me on a regular basis, as if I were their child. I found refuge in their kindness, and I hoped that, in some way, they found refuge in me.

One Saturday morning a few months after Mason's death, Judy called and asked me to come by.

"Sure," I said. "See you soon." I didn't ask why.

As was the norm, I let myself in. Mason's mother was sitting on the living room sofa with her Bible open on the table in front of her. She offered me a cup of coffee before going to the kitchen. I loved when she made me coffee—it reminded me of the Sundays when Mason and I stayed together at her house and she would bring it to me in bed.

While waiting for her to return, I watched the dust particles dance in the sun streaming through the window, and reminisced about the last night I had with Mason. We had been right there on that same sofa talking about our future.

I jumped when his mother placed the coffee on the table in front of me.

"Were you thinking of Mason?"

I smiled. "Yeah."

She returned my smile as she put her own cup down beside her Bible. Judy sat for a few minutes before picking up her cup for a sip of her drink. That's when I noticed an ever so slight tremble of her hand. She was nervous, and that made me nervous.

186

"Tina, I asked you over here today because God wants me to apologize and ask for your forgiveness."

Heat rushed to my face as I began to sweat. I held my breath, watching her struggle for words—but I offered no help, struggling myself.

Finally, she spoke. "It's my fault you didn't get to say goodbye to Mason."

I allowed myself to let my breath out. I sat quietly and listened, my breathing shallow as she continued. "I was so angry and terrified that day, and I took hold of the only thing I had control of—who got to see Mason." She took a sip of tea and cleared her throat. "He begged me to let you in the hospital room so he could tell you how much he loved you. He said he thought it would destroy you if he didn't get to say goodbye. But I let my anger over what had happened between the two of you and my fear of losing him forever control my decisions that day instead of following Jesus's promptings. I can never take back what I did, but I hope you can come to forgive me."

I didn't know what to say and thought I must seem cold or angry. After all, she had just lost her son. But the more I thought about it, the more I realized that I *was* angry. I wondered why she was telling me this now, and what she expected me to do with the guilt she'd laid at my feet. Did she think I was better off knowing that Mason had desperately wanted to see me in his last moments? I couldn't stop imagining how powerless he must have felt when she denied him his dying wish. It made me feel rage.

"I forgive you," I said as I leaned in to hug her, suddenly desperate to leave.

As we held each other, my urgent need to escape dissolved. As angry as I was, I hadn't realized how much I needed to hear her say she was sorry. I was realizing it now. The truth stung, but it was brave of her to tell it.

Mason was still gone, but I had his family back.

Chapter 31

Let it Go

Mason's death sparked thoughts about my mother's. I found myself wanting to know the truth. I needed answers to questions I had avoided for nearly ten years.

First, I thought over everything I knew—how my mother suddenly wanted a gun, then just as suddenly wanted to give it back to my father. How Brandy and my father guarded my mother's hospital room like something was going to get out. How the obvious tension grew between Brandy and my father in the days following my mother's death. The rumor that some girl had climbed out of my mother's bedroom window the day she was shot. And I wondered, would my mother, a devout Christian, really kill herself? And if she had—why? She had seemed fairly optimistic the last time we saw each other. She had hopes and dreams for me, ones I knew she wanted to see come true. With all my thoughts organized, what I needed now was real evidence.

My investigation began with Francis and Virgil, the elderly couple that had been her close friends. I hadn't seen them since my mother's funeral, but I had no trouble finding them. They lived in the same house in Oak Cliff where they'd been when my mother was alive. It was a small, light red brick house, with a narrow one car driveway with only enough concrete for the tires. There were three steps to the door that had an oval-shaped frosted window in its center.

"Tina!" Francis cried, as she threw her arms around me and walked me inside the house. "Virgil, look who's here, all grown up."

I hugged Virgil and sat down on the living room sofa. Francis sat beside me, and Virgil took a seat across from us.

"We got your high school graduation invitation. Jody would have been so proud, Tina," Francis said. "I'm sorry we couldn't make it, but we got you a gift. We weren't sure how to get it to you." She stood and hurried off to another room.

Francis returned with a small box. "I've been saving this for you, and hoped you would come by one day. I'm so glad that day has come."

I opened the gift to find a beautiful silver bracelet with sapphire stones and a note that read, *Your mother would be proud.* It almost made me cry.

Being there with them was easy; it made me feel close to my mother in a way I hadn't felt for a long time. We talked about our lives. I shared all I'd been through with Mason's death and the aftermath. They shared stories about my mother and their friendship, some things I'd never heard before. I could tell how much they adored her.

The emotions were overwhelming, but I needed to know what they thought about my mother's death. I wondered whether they believed she killed herself. I didn't know how to ask. I took a deep breath and began.

"You know, I remember walking by my mother's hospital room before they let me in. You were sitting with her and holding her hand. Did she tell you what happened?"

Neither of them spoke. Instead, they looked at each other. When Virgil finally nodded, Francis turned to me.

"We could never confirm the truth, Tina. When we visited Jody in the hospital, we couldn't ask her openly because your father and Brandy stood in the doorway watching. But when we stood up to leave, I bent down to hug her and whispered in her ear, 'Jody, who shot you?' She couldn't answer because of the ventilator, but tears ran down her face as she slowly turned to look at your father standing at the door. That's when your father asked if she wanted to see you. At that moment, I was certain he had shot her." Francis put her head in her hands and began to sob.

Virgil picked up where she left off. "Tina, we are so sorry we didn't go to the police. We were afraid he'd kill us too. Before she was shot, Jody told us she was fearful your father was going to kill her. That's why she decided to move back to El Paso. She'd been talking to her son and sister and was excited about reuniting with them. She sold her beauty shop to Lupe and was leaving in a few days."

Francis stood and knelt in front of me. She grabbed both my hands, looked me in the eye, and said, "Tina, Jody loved you very much—she was coming back for you. *She was coming back for you.*"

THE NEXT DAY, I went to the police station and the lady at the front desk printed off the one-page incident report concerning my mother's death. There was one paragraph summarizing what happened that day. The two officers on the report still worked for the Dallas Police Department, and I left each of them a message.

Officer Denny called me back a week later. I started talking as soon as he introduced himself. "You were the first responder to a scene back in May of 1981—my mother had been shot. I know it was a long time ago, but I was wondering if you would tell me what happened that day."

He cleared his throat. "I knew I'd get this call someday. Yes, I

190

remember it like it happened yesterday. I'll never forget it. How can I help you?"

"Can you tell me everything you remember?"

"Okay," he said after a moment, "but only if you're really sure you want to go down this road."

"Yes, please tell me everything," I said, trying not to sound too eager.

"Okay," he said, taking in a deep breath. "I was just a rookie then, only had my badge a few months. I was on the way to my beat, which was on the other side of Oak Cliff, when the call came through. I responded because I was only a block away. When I pulled up, I saw your father pacing outside the house, mumbling, 'She shot herself.' As I questioned your father, I realized his time-line didn't make sense. It took him forty-five minutes to call 911. When I asked him why it took so long, he just said he was in shock and didn't know what to do. But he also couldn't tell me what he'd been doing during that forty-five minutes. My superior officer arrived about five minutes later, and after I told him what your father said, he ordered me to leave. I asked him if I should write up a report based on what your father told me. 'No, I got this,' he said. 'I said you can go.' I said, 'Okay, Sarge, but I think something is off about that guy and this whole scene.' On the way to my car, I pulled the sergeant aside one last time and suggested we have your mother tested for gunshot residue on her hand. All he said was 'We've got this, and I told you to leave.' It really bothered me, Tina, and still does to this day." He paused as though he needed a moment to collect himself and then continued.

"Once the reports were completed, I reviewed them. No one ever tested your mother's hands for gunshot residue. Your father tested negative, but the testing was done at the station several hours later. Have you seen a copy of the police report?"

"Yes," I managed to say.

"The sergeant barely did a report, let alone an investigation. Tina, I am so sorry I didn't do more. I was a rookie and scared to challenge a superior. I have regretted it all these years. In fact, it has haunted me. I'm hoping by telling you all of this, it will help bring you closure. But please understand, if anyone finds out I spoke to you, I could lose my badge, pension—everything. I have a wife and two little girls."

With sniffles, I said, "I won't say anything," But I immediately thought, *how will I get to the truth if I don't say anything—why did I tell him that?*

"Just know that after what happened that day, I never ignored anything again and took heat when I needed to in order to do the right thing."

"Officer Denny, you can let this go now," I said softly, despite the whirlwind of emotions inside me. "It doesn't need to haunt you. What you've shared with me today—it's exactly what I needed. The truth. And for that, I will be forever grateful."

After the call ended, I sat there, tears slipping down my face as I processed it all. I cried for a few minutes mulling it over. I felt in my heart that what he had told me was the truth—something about the emotion in his voice. But logically it didn't make sense—he said he could lose his job if anyone found out he talked to me. Did he really just trust a nineteen-year-old girl with information that could ruin his career or was this a plan to keep me quiet?

I took a deep breath and dialed the police station, again.

I needed to talk to Denny's superior officer, Sergeant White. They said he wasn't there. I called again the next day, and the day after that. I kept calling for the next two weeks, until I finally got him on the phone. He seemed to know exactly who I was.

"Listen, young lady, that was nearly ten years ago, and I'm retiring soon. I don't remember anything, and I can't help you. Don't call me again!" He yelled, slamming the phone down.

I stared at the receiver in my shaking hand. I wanted to call him back, but decided it was safer not to. Officer Denny's confession and Sergeant White's defensive tone and irrational anger were enough to confirm what I already knew in my heart.

Still, I wasn't done with my investigation. I wanted to know everything. I sent a formal request for my mother's medical records to Parkland Hospital. Three weeks and multiple phone calls later, I got the call I'd been waiting for—the records were ready.

The next day, I drove an hour to Parkland. After searching for the records department for more than twenty minutes, I finally tracked down a custodian who directed me to the basement.

There, sitting behind the open top half of a wooden door, was an older woman wearing red-rimmed glasses. When I told her why I was there, she went to a file cabinet and returned to her desk with an armful of papers. She shuffled through them, and then handed me a short stack, paper-clipped together.

"Five pages?" I asked, confused. "She was in the hospital for several days." I waved the papers at her. "This is all you have?"

She looked at me and shrugged. I waited for more, but she ignored me. As far as she was concerned, I was already gone.

I took the records home and scanned every word, looking for clues as to what happened the day my mother was shot. On the last page, there was a tiny note made by the EMT that read:

"AS WE LOADED THE PATIENT ONTO THE BUS, SHE STATED: 'I DON'T KNOW WHY THEY WANT TO HURT ME NO I DON'T CAUSE HES THE FATHER OF MY KIDS.'"

THERE IT WAS—EVIDENCE she didn't shoot herself. I called the Dallas Police Department and demanded to speak to whoever was in charge of my mother's case. He wasn't there anymore. When the detective, Jim Bryan, finally called me back, we made an appointment to talk in person.

The next week, I followed Detective Bryan into a room and he closed the door. "How old are you, young lady?"

"Nineteen. But about to be twenty."

"Tell me what I can do for you."

I told him everything I knew and showed him the notes from the EMT. I never said a word about Officer Denny. Detective Bryan agreed to order my mother's file from storage. He said it would take a week or two for the boxes to arrive and that he would call me. I left feeling hopeful that I might get some answers. The truth was all that mattered.

Two weeks later, I still hadn't heard from him. I called and left a message. A few days later, I called and left another message. For three weeks, I called twice a day, leaving messages, but he wouldn't return my call.

The following week, I took a vacation day and drove nearly an hour to downtown Dallas to confront him in person.

"He's out of the office," the blonde receptionist said.

"When will he be back?"

She stepped out before answering and returned a few minutes later with another lady.

"We don't know when Detective Bryan will return," the new brunette lady said.

"Well, I took a vacation day. So I'll just wait right here until he comes back."

I sat in the waiting area for several hours before he finally came out to get me. For all I knew, he had been there the whole time.

"Why haven't you returned my calls?" I asked as soon as we got to his desk that was in a big open room. "What is going on? I thought you were going to help me get to the truth."

He sighed. "Look, we got the boxes, and it appears they were stored in a building that caught fire. The records have some water damage—and my boss decided not to reopen the case."

"I thought you said it sounded like maybe it wasn't properly investigated." I was growing angrier with each word he said.

"Tina, I don't think it was, but it's out of my hands. I'm sorry."

I stood abruptly. "I want to see the file then, if you won't tell me what happened."

Detective Bryan looked around as he put his hand on my shoulder and slowly guided me back down into the chair. "You have to calm down and lower your voice," he whispered. "I don't want to show you the pictures. They're bad, and you shouldn't see them."

"Okay, then explain to me again why you aren't going to properly investigate," I shot back. "You said you would. Why did you go through the trouble of ordering the boxes if you weren't going to do anything?"

He shrugged. "I don't know why my boss said no."

I glared at him with my arms crossed. Tears had started to fall.

He leaned in toward me and whispered. "Tina, what do you want to gain from this?"

"I want to know the truth," I said, standing up.

He again coaxed me back into the chair. "I think you are right —that he did it—but do you really want your father to go to jail now?"

I leaned my elbows on his desk and looked straight into his eyes. "If he killed her, then he should go to jail."

"Okay, okay. I'll talk to my superiors again," he said, shaking his head. "That's all I can do."

For weeks, I obsessed over the answers I thought I needed. I called the detective repeatedly, but he wouldn't respond. I replayed everything I knew in my head on an endless loop.

Then, one night, I dreamed of my mother. I was ten and nineteen at the same time. She lay in a hospital bed, surrounded by a golden glow, wearing a white satin gown with delicate lace lining the neckline and sleeves. Young Tina sat beside her on a small stool, holding her hand. Teenager Tina stood in the doorway watching them. The child smiled, nodding as my mother spoke to her, but I —at nineteen—couldn't hear their words. I just watched as my mother kissed young Tina's hand.

195

When my mother finally looked up at me, I ran to her bedside. "Mama," I said. "It's not fair. He can't get away with this."

"Just let it go, *mija*. Let it go," she said, her voice gentle but firm, as she took my hand. "It won't change anything." She smiled softly and smoothed my hair back. "Go live your life. Be happy."

I woke abruptly, sitting straight up in my bed, her words echoing in my head. Tears streamed down my face uncontrollably, my heart pounding. I knew then—without a doubt—that it was a message from my mother. My investigation was over. The only justice I could give her was to live my life in a way that would make her proud.

Chapter 32

Just Friends

Quincy and I met through Casey, a mutual friend. Casey had just started a new job, and Quincy was the owner's son. They quickly became friends, and the next thing I knew, Casey had invited Quincy to join us in Copeville—a place when I was younger thought was called Cokeville because an old dude who lived there threw lots of parties with lots of drugs.

Walking up the driveway to the old white farmhouse, I could hear "Dark Side of the Moon" playing and could see strobe lights through the windows. I'd taken a couple of shots before I left the house, but I was ready for another drink after the hour-long drive. I ran into Casey in the kitchen. "There she is!" Casey yelled across the crowded room, lifting his cup toward me. He was already tipsy.

He introduced me to Quincy, the guy standing next to him. He was a little taller than Casey, who wasn't quite six feet tall, and had a blonde mullet and blue eyes. "You kids have fun," Casey told us after we'd said our hellos.

Quincy had his hands in his pockets, looking around the room and avoiding direct eye contact. I made small talk and asked him how he knew Casey. He explained what I already knew, that they worked together as mechanics. Quincy went on to tell me about an old pickup he was restoring. I saw Mary and her boyfriend, George, across the room. Our eyes met and I gave her the look to come save me, and she did.

Quincy listened to us talk, laughing when appropriate, but didn't say much. He left to find the bathroom and we took off outside. I had learned how to walk a party. I kept my eye on him and when he moved closer, I'd wait a minute or so and I'd move further away.

Casey caught me in the hallway. "Why are you ignoring Quincy?"

"Because he won't stop following me around."

"I told him this was a date."

I hit him on the arm. "Dude, that's so wrong."

"Go hang out and have fun, Tina. You deserve it."

I had to admit the attention was flattering. I wasn't looking to date. But the emptiness I felt was unbearable at times. Maybe a distraction would be good for me. So, I gave in and found Quincy. We played drinking games, shot pool, and danced until it was nearly daylight.

After a month of phone calls, Quincy finally wore me down and convinced me to go on an actual date with him. Then he won me over. The way he adored me reminded me of Mason, and the attention felt good. Quincy initiated phone calls and planned dates. Before long, we had settled into a comfortable groove as a couple. He did all the work while I went along for the ride.

Being in a stable relationship with Quincy, gave me emotional space to think about my future again. I began taking part-time night classes at the local community college. My advisor told me that my test scores showed that I could barely read on a tenth-grade level, and remedial classes would be mandatory. I'd missed so much school in my younger years, it was no wonder I was academically behind compared to other students my age.

One day, in the spring of 1991, as I was sitting in the commercial drive-thru lane at the bank, waiting for the teller to return my receipt, I had a thought: maybe I could be a bank teller. I could feel the blood in my veins pumping a little faster. Instead of running around smelling like greasy chicken, I'd be standing behind a counter doling out money. And gone would be my hideous blue and tan uniform.

So I applied. And got the job.

My KFC friends ridiculed me for taking a huge pay cut so I could focus on taking night classes that would take nearly a decade to finish at the pace I was going. But our forty-five-year-old area manager, who had been working at KFC for twenty years, had just been replaced with someone who had a college degree. I could see the writing on the wall.

A few weeks later, I started working as a bank teller in the drive-thru. It felt odd to be sitting in a chair, waiting for the next customer, instead of cleaning or stocking items in between slow periods. But I quickly got used to it and used the downtime to study.

It was my second year of night classes, and things were going well. With more time for studying while at work, I made better grades. While I liked the stability of the hours, the money wasn't enough—I was short four hundred dollars every month. I reached out to my previous KFC boss and asked to work on Sundays. The extra money helped with groceries, and I could take food home at the end of the night.

But Quincy wasn't happy with my decision. Sunday was his only day off. Six months later, he asked me to quit KFC. By then I had been eating dinner at his house most nights and he insisted I didn't need a second job anymore. It was true that his mother's home cooking was wonderful, but I needed a break from him. A year into dating, if I wasn't at work or college, I was with Quincy. I barely even saw my friends—which I convinced myself was a good thing. At the same time, I enjoyed time away from him and I was feeling suffocated.

One day during Christmas break, Quincy and I had finished dinner with his parents and went to his room to relax. His parents had converted their dining room into a huge bedroom for him, and he had a blue sofa with puffy cushions and rounded arms made of wood.

We were sitting on the sofa for a few minutes, and he didn't turn on the television, which was strange—watching TV on that sofa after dinner had become our routine.

And then he popped the question.

"When I graduate high school in May, let's move in together."

"I'm not ready for that," I said without hesitation. "I like what we have now."

"But I love you, and I just want to be with you."

"The only way I'd consider moving in together is if we're married," I insisted, thinking that at eighteen, he'd never go for that.

My plan backfired. After he graduated high school, I had a ring on my finger. Even though I felt smothered and didn't love Quincy the way I should, I told myself that he had a loving family that I fit into well, and my life was truly stable, for once. I convinced myself that would be enough.

Chapter 33

Love, Marriage, Therapy

One night after dinner, Quincy's mother was standing at her mustard yellow kitchen sink washing dishes. I was clearing off the dinner table that sat between the kitchen and living room area and could see the television in the living room—it was surrounded by a massive brown wooden entertainment shelving system, so was kind of hard to miss. Quincy and his father and brother were watching *Home Improvement*.

I carried over the last few dishes to his mother, who was shorter than me, with salt and pepper short wavy hair. She smiled, showing her dimples, and said, "I could make your wedding dress if you wanted, and it would save you and Quincy a lot of money."

"Oh, wow—you can sew! That would be wonderful. Are you sure you don't mind?"

She hesitated for a second and said, "Well, it's a big endeavor for one person. How would you feel about helping me?"

"If you don't mind teaching me, sure, but I'm not very good at that kind of stuff."

"I'd love to teach you. I've always wanted a daughter and now I have one." Quincy came running into the kitchen in his socks. As he slid to a stop, he kissed me on the cheek and said, "Mom, what's for dessert?"

Her question triggered memories of my mother sewing on her beloved sewing machine, and the joy it brought watching her smile and hum a tune. She would even sometimes let me press the pedal. The noise of the oven opening and the smell of pineapple upside-down cake snapped me back to the present, reminding me of where I actually was, and that my mother was gone.

TWO WEEKS LATER, Quincy's mother asked if I was ready to work on the wedding dress. I had been putting it off. I think she saw my hesitation in getting started, but neither of us said a word acknowledging that. That was how Quincy's family operated, and for the time being, I was good with it.

I let Quincy's mom take over the planning because all of my friends had married in Vegas or at the courthouse, I had zero experience in that department. I'd never been to a real wedding and I didn't have the first clue of how to plan one, nor did I especially want to. My anxiety increased as we made more plans.

ONE WEEK BEFORE THE WEDDING, it was nearly time for me to leave Quincy's house so I could go home and get ready for bed. We were sitting on the sofa in his bedroom watching *Star Trek the Next Generation*. During each commercial break, I tried to find the courage to tell him my true feelings. Finally, I blurted it out, "I'm sorry, Quincy. I can't marry you. I don't love you the way I should, and it's not fair to you."

I slipped the ring off my finger and gently placed it on his leg.

He sat up straight and took the ring with his right hand, "I know you don't love me the same way I love you, but I love you enough for the both of us," he said, gently taking my left hand to put the ring back on my finger.

I soon realized there wasn't going to be quick and easy way out of this.

We talked for a whole hour. He cried and begged me not to back out. I relented.

A week later, as Mason's father escorted me down the aisle, I felt certain I was making a huge mistake, but the train was moving full speed ahead, and I couldn't see a way stop the locomotive.

Quincy and I had only been married eighteen months when I told him I wanted a divorce. We had married too young, and neither of us married for love. He had wanted out of his parents' house, and I had wanted financial stability. He didn't see it that way, but we needed to face the facts and move on.

We were both working full-time and attending community college at night. Superficially, things were great. On the weekends, we'd ride jet skis and dirt bikes, go camping with friends, or have friends over to play cards. I was finally enjoying life rather than merely trying to survive. Even still, I periodically battled suicidal thoughts that I never disclosed to anyone for fear of being ridiculed and possibly being committed to a mental hospital.

At twenty-three, I had been working and going to school for ten years. I was exhausted. I was carrying around deep-seated despair and sadness that I couldn't manage. Nobody saw that— what they did see was the part of me that protected myself from all danger. I had an angry monster inside of me that appeared whenever I needed her. In one of those moments, a friend said to the group, "Remind me not to piss Tina off." Everyone had laughed. I realized I'd heard that same line many times over the years and proudly owned those words. But this time, it hit me differently—I didn't feel proud.

When I broke the news, Quincy's eyes filled with tears and he begged me to go to counseling before resorting to divorce. Reluctantly, I agreed, and after a couple of joint sessions, Karla told us we each needed individual sessions. At the end of my session alone with Karla, I learned that I'd never grieved my childhood and had only then realized that I needed to.

Karla's office had a plush loveseat and a winged-back chair. I chose the loveseat. She settled into her office chair opposite me with a yellow pad and pen in her hand, ready to start. Each weekly session started the same. We'd sit down and she'd say, "What do you want to work on today?"

I would respond with "Nothing, so you pick."

I dug deeper into my childhood trauma, peeling back layers of pain and buried memories.

Part of the counseling process involved confronting the pain of being abandoned, abused, and neglected—the things that had happened to "Little Tina," the version of myself I had buried deep inside. Facing those memories was difficult and strange. It meant talking to an empty chair, imagining myself speaking to the child I once was, and confronting the pain I had long tried to hide.

Even worse, Quincy had no interest in hearing about my counseling sessions, much less any of my childhood trauma. Staying in my marriage was beginning to feel less and less desirable, and therapy felt useless. If anything, things between us had only gotten worse. I was ready to throw in the towel when Karla asked if I'd be open to trying an alternative approach.

At that point, I would have done anything to stop talking to a pillow in a chair that Karla urged me to think of as "Little Tina."

EMDR was weird too, but several sessions later, I wasn't dreading the visit with Karla as much as I had been. Something had shifted, urging me to continue.

That first year of therapy was intense—like clinging to the edge of a cliff waiting for a rescue helicopter that might never come. I became severely depressed and found it hard to keep going. Karla suggested antidepressants, but in my circle of friends, only the weak took those kinds of pills, and I had bought into that idea too. In Texas, we're taught to pick ourselves up by our bootstraps. We didn't take medicine or whine to some stranger about all our problems.

Quincy refused to go to individual counseling, and sometimes, I could hardly bring myself to go. Death seemed an easier option than facing the reality of my present situation, while also dealing with my past. In those moments, I'd cry out to God for the strength to keep going. And then I would remember that promise I made so long ago: "God, if you get me out of this house alive, I promise I'll make something of myself." I couldn't break my promise.

Chapter 34

The Truth Comes Out

W hen I first began attending night classes, I had thought an accountant would be a good profession for me. Then six months after starting my first accounts-receivable position, my boss came to me and said, "You're great at your job, but you don't love it. You should find something that excites you." I followed her advice and changed my major.

I graduated from the University of North Texas with a bachelor's degree in criminal justice and a minor in business administration in May of 1997. The job search began, and with a degree, the opportunities seemed endless.

I imagined being in a high-power position someday, wearing a navy blue pantsuit and making big decisions from my office with a view of the Dallas skyline. After work, I would get in my expensive, shiny black car and drive to an even fancier restaurant, where Quincy and I would dine with my colleagues and their spouses. That was a nice little dream. But I knew I needed to start at the bottom of the totem pole.

Although I was still working at the bank, my eyes kept landing on the legal section of the *Dallas Morning News* classifieds. Obviously, I couldn't be a lawyer, but maybe I could work for one. There was only one problem with that idea—law firms required at least two years of experience to apply for the paralegal positions, and would they conduct a background check? Would my juvenile record be revealed?

Reality hit me in the face. It seemed I would never be free from my past and I might have to settle for climbing the ladder at the bank. I began praying for the right job to come along. I wanted to be in the legal field more than anything—but I was starting to think that was just a pipe dream.

A few weeks later, during my usual employment search, a new position caught my eye. *Downtown Dallas mid-size Law Firm seeking legal assistant, no experience necessary. Four-year degree required.* There it was in black and white, the job of my dreams—I wasn't sure what being a legal assistant meant, but I didn't care.

The employment application asked if I had been "convicted of a crime" and I checked the box "no." Because technically, juveniles are not convicted—they are adjudicated. During the interview, there were no questions regarding criminal history, and I didn't offer up details about my juvenile escapades.

I HAD ALWAYS worried about my past coming back to haunt me, and one day, six months after I had been working at the law firm, in October of that year, the reckoning happened.

"Tina, why don't you go to law school? You'd make a great lawyer."

I looked up to see Jean, a young associate at the law firm, standing in the doorway to my office. He was waiting for a response. I said the same thing I'd rehearsed for a while: "It's just not in the cards for me."

Jean stepped inside, closed the door, and sat down in one of the brown chairs across from my desk. "Tina, tell me the real reason why you aren't going to law school."

Everybody at the office had been telling me I'd be a good lawyer and should go to law school. It didn't help that the two previous employees that had my job went to law school.

No one had pressed me like this. No one cared enough, and I wasn't sure why Jean did. We were friendly, but he was a lawyer, and I was a legal assistant. Support staff didn't mingle too much with the lawyers. My arm pits were suddenly wet and my face warm. I was stuck, maybe he already knew. *I really thought this job was from God, but I'm about to be fired.*

Now, here was Jean, sitting across from me and waiting for my answer. As terrified as I was that everyone would know my secret, I was even more tired of hiding.

"I got into trouble when I was fifteen and I have a felony charge on my record," I blurted out.

Jean looked at me and then the ceiling. I had become very good at reading people, but I couldn't read him. After a few seconds, without saying a word, he got up and walked out.

I turned around in my chair and looked out my office window, knowing it would be the last day I could enjoy the beautiful view of downtown Dallas. Jean had certainly gone to tell the senior partners my secret. Soon, I would be escorted out of the office. I began organizing my projects in separate stacks on my desk, making notes of what needed to be done for each stack so they wouldn't miss any deadlines.

Twenty minutes later, Jean returned holding a large, open black book in his hands. He plopped it down on my desk and pointed to a section. "Tina, go get your record expunged," he demanded, turning around and walking out the door.

"What are you talking about?"

He spoke from the doorway. "It's all right there. Read it. And if you need any help, let me know, but it's pretty easy. You can do it."

I read the page he pointed to three or four times, sitting there in disbelief, waiting for the reality of the situation to set in. Not only was I not getting fired—I could finally put the past behind me and maybe even be a lawyer someday.

I was so excited, I left early and went home to tell Quincy the good news. I began talking as soon as I walked into the house, which wasn't unusual for me.

"I found out today that I might actually be able to become a lawyer."

"Then that's what you should do." Quincy may have had his shortcomings, but he never failed to support my crazy endeavors.

"I don't know. It seems like a lot," I said. I was beginning to feel deflated by the ideas swarming in my head. "I'm too old to go to law school, and we can't afford it."

He grabbed my hand. "If you really want to do this, we'll do it together."

"Really, Quincy? Are you serious?" His little push of support suddenly made me feel braver. "Oh my God, I can't believe this might happen."

He laughed as I started jumping up and down with excitement. "Let's get dinner and figure out the first step. I can't wait to be a stay-at-home husband."

Chapter 35

Acceptance

The law school entrance exam would decide my fate. I was a horrible test taker, but knew I only had to do well enough to get into one law school—somewhere—and hoped that God would take care of the rest. Lawyers at the office suggested I take the Kaplan LSAT prep course to help me score higher on the test. To my surprise, I scored ten points higher than my practice exams—but it was not a great score, to say the least.

A few months had passed since I mailed my five law school applications. One evening at work, my mind kept drifting back to law school and the endless what-ifs. I took a brief break, gazing out my office window as the sun set behind a tall skyscraper. My office was a common stopping point for the lawyers on their way to the restroom, and they often teased me about my law school plans.

As one of the older attorneys walked by on his way to the men's room, he paused and asked, "Ready to read a hundred pages a night?"

I turned around to look at him and responded with a nervous laugh. "Fake it till you make it, right?" I said a little sheepishly.

With his hands in his pockets, and without a word, he smiled, nodded, and walked away.

As silly as it might sound, I hadn't thought about how much reading I was going to have to do. Suddenly, memories of struggling with reading comprehension in high school and undergrad haunted me. At twenty-seven years old, the only book I'd read cover to cover was *A Tale of Two Cities*. I needed a plan to solve this problem and thought getting more involved in church and reading the Bible more could help.

I began attending a women's bible study and shared my concerns with them about keeping up with the rigid reading schedule in law school. One night after bible study, a retired high school English teacher approached me. "Find a speed-reading book," she told me. "Practice what you learn in that book, and you'll be just fine." Her voice was soothing, and her advice resonated with me. I found the book she recommended and got to reading. Having something to focus on daily while waiting for an acceptance letter helped ease the trepidation I had been feeling. I spent the next several months reading more than I had in the last ten years of my life.

MY FIRST LAW school acceptance letter arrived on a sunny spring day in 1998. I ripped open the unexpected envelope that came from a law school in Nebraska that I hadn't even applied to— Creighton University School of Law. I had already received rejections from both Texas law schools I'd applied to and had been praying for an acceptance letter from the last two schools in California.

The letter from Creighton explained that, after reviewing my credentials from the Law School Admission Council, they wanted to offer me admission to their law school.

Days later, a second acceptance letter arrived from Quinnipiac University School of Law and they offered me a thirty-thousand-dollar scholarship. I wanted to go somewhere different and the East Coast sounded exciting, but Quincy preferred to stay closer to his family. The only way to make Creighton workable would be through financial assistance. After a twenty-minute phone call to the assistant dean, Creighton matched Connecticut's scholarship offer and I ended the call, we scheduled a visit to Omaha for the following month.

Omaha was quaint and much smaller than I had anticipated. As we drove up to the campus, the trees swayed gently, their leaves rustling in the breeze. We wandered the halls with the assistant dean, and the students and professors stopped to speak to us, asking questions and graciously sharing their wisdom. I felt an immediate connection to the energy of the law school. The transition between classes and the peaceful quiet that followed was surreal. The brand-new library had a fresh smell and featured an abundance of cherry-red shelves filled with more books than I'd ever seen. The wall of windows offered views of a serene landscape that surrounded the campus. By the end of the visit, I knew this was where I belonged.

THREE MONTHS before I would be leaving for law school, I received a letter from my sister Brandy—she had been in and out of prison for drugs for nearly fifteen years and she was about to be paroled out. She asked to live with me and Quincy. I knew she didn't really have anywhere else to go.

Thoughts of the last time I lived with her came rushing back.

My father had dropped me off at her house for two weeks when I was eleven years old. She and her baby's father were living two houses down from my mother's house. Brandy's baby was about six months old. I called her JJ. Her parents sat in the living room with needles, spoons, and drugs while she cried for a solid hour that first day. Brandy kept saying, "Nothing I do works—she'll eventually stop crying."

I finally caved and went to see if I could do something—anything to make the shrilling noise stop. I'd seen in movies that checking the diaper was the first thing to do and, sure enough, that was it. A few minutes later, it started again, and I went to find a bottle of formula. I'd never changed a diaper or fed a baby, but all those years of watching television had helped prepare me.

The first day or two, it was difficult to console JJ, but I finally figured out that carrying her around, feeding and changing her often, and wiping her down with a warm, wet rag did the trick. I'd sometimes sing the "Hush Little Baby" lullaby to her. She would smile, coo, and fall asleep. Then I would sigh with relief. After two weeks, she was much easier to manage.

That was when my father showed up.

We ended up taking her with us and had her for a month or so until one of my cousins took her to Ohio to live with her father's parents. The phone rang and snapped me back to reality—I finished reading Brandy's letter.

I had received a few letters over the years, but I wasn't expecting the request she made in this one. "Dear Tina, I know it has been a long time, and I haven't been a good sister, but I'm hoping you will give me a chance to be a better one." I felt tears well up. "I'm coming up for parole in August and I need a stable place to live. Can I parole out to you and Quincy?"

My heart sank, and I sat on the sofa and leaned my head back, closing my eyes. I began to pray. *I don't know what to do. I need a sign, God, please. Something to tell me what to do.* And then I remembered the bible story about Peter asking Jesus how many times he should forgive his brother. Jesus answered, "I tell you, not seven times, but seventy-seven times." The answer that came to me —my "sign"—was that I didn't need one.

As much as I wanted to move forward with my new life, I knew that I was all Brandy had and felt pretty sure I was supposed to help her. At thirty-four, I reasoned, surely she was truly ready to leave the drugs behind for good. But Quincy would have to agree. I had to find a way to tell him about Brandy's letter. I was scared to approach him—it was a big ask, after all.

The timing couldn't have been better, it felt like divine intervention. As we sat down to eat, he brought up his post-graduation plans, a topic that had been a sore spot between us for months.

"With a history degree, all I could really do is teach and I don't want to do that," he said. "I had a thought—I really enjoyed the business law class I took last semester and I've been thinking about going to law school."

I nearly spit my coke all over him before saying, "Law school?"

"Yeah, he mumbled, head down, shoveling food into his mouth. I've been thinking about it for a while but wanted to be sure before I told you."

Well, that was pretty responsible of him, I thought. But how would we pay for his law school education? Would he even finish? And we would have so much student loan debt.

"Quincy, you've always supported me and my crazy endeavors over the years, and if that is what you really want to do, we'll make it work."

"Yes, I promise this is what I want to do," he said, like a child who had just gotten permission to take care of the new cat they were going to adopt.

That seemed like the perfect time to tell him about Brandy's letter. After telling him, he said, "What if you asked Creighton for permission to start next August instead of in three months? We could be in law school at the same time—it would be so cool."

"I guess, I could ask Creighton to let me defer a year?"

"Tina, maybe this is a sign from God that we are supposed to help Brandy?"

"Okay, okay. You've convinced me, I'll call Monday."

I spoke with the assistant dean. She told me I'd have to apply for admission for the 1999 class and that she couldn't make any promises. I would later learn that was a phrase all lawyers liked to use—and often. Still, I figured that, if this was God's plan, it would all work out.

Chapter 36

Reckoning

I postponed law school for one year and wrote Brandy a letter excited to share the good news. At the end of August, she showed up on our doorstep, fresh out of prison. We decorated her bedroom, bought her an old car, and some clothes. Despite giving her everything we could, to set her up for success, a month later, she left one morning and never came back. My rage at her, my life, and God's repeated disappointments flooded through me, consuming my whole body. I had no choice but to deal with my emotions.

I had been working hard in therapy, getting mentally prepared for law school, but now our focus had to shift to processing the disappointment of Brandy's decision. It only took a few sessions to work through the anger. That's when Karla, always able to find a silver lining, suggested I use the next year to get to know my father.

I had spent years avoiding the topic of him, keeping any mention of our relationship or lack thereof at bay. And now she wanted me to spend quality time with him? She had to be out of her mind!

"There's so much you don't know about your mother and her

side of the family, and you never will," Karla said, taking a moment to pause. "And if you don't talk with your father, you'll never know anything about his side either—I worry that later in life, you might want to know where you came from and it'll be too late."

I couldn't even remember the last time we had spoken—maybe right after Mason died? And as weird as it was, my father only lived two miles away. I passed his street every time I drove to Quincy's parents' house. It was a constant reminder of the distance between us. That, along with my promise to Karla, was what finally set this first visit in motion.

My hands shook as I waited on my father's front porch, trying to summon the courage to knock. Taking in a deep breath, I tapped on the door three times. My body tensed when I heard approaching footsteps from inside.

A moment later, my father opened the door and stood there with his mouth wide open. He took a step back, making way for me to enter.

"You're the last person I expected to see when I opened this door, baby doll."

I shrugged, despite my pounding heart. "Got any coffee?" I asked, moving past him and into the house.

Everything looked the same as it did ten years ago when I crawled out of my bedroom window. I walked through the living room, past the same couch to the right and the same old television on the left, and made my way to the kitchen table. Nan shuffled around in the laundry room while my father made a pot of coffee.

And then, there I was sitting across from the man I had once feared and hated more than anybody else. He picked up the newspaper, flipping it open like I wasn't even there. I tried to think of something to say—anything—but the words wouldn't come. I kept glancing over my shoulder at the old brown cuckoo clock next to the back door. It was ugly yet familiar. Although I had arrived at eight-forty-five, the clock only read five after nine. Twenty minutes. That was all the time that had passed. But I had made a promise to Karla to stay for one hour, and I was determined to keep it.

At nine forty-five, I jumped to my feet and said, "Gotta go," I took my coffee cup to the sink. "Church is starting soon." I rushed toward the front door.

My father stood, obviously looking for a hug, as I hurried past him.

"I'll see you in a couple of weeks. Bye, Nan," I said before opening the door and walking onto the porch. I kept my promise to Karla.

Over the next year, I visited my father twice a month on Sundays, then processed it with Karla if necessary. Over time, I started to understand him better. Apparently, he had to grow up quickly too. He'd been picking cotton since he was six years old, but at fifteen when his father died, he had to get a real job. Someone had to support his mother and sister—his older siblings had married and left the house.

He told me a story about serving on the front lines in Korea. One night, his best friend got caught in the barbed wire and spent hours crying out, "Dub, please come help me." But my father couldn't help him, or he would have been killed too. He also described watching his platoon leader put a bullet in his own head out of guilt for losing his entire platoon—with the exception of my father. To survive in the freezing cold, he dug a foxhole and stayed in there for a few days, until another army unit found him. He had lied about his age to enlist, and at only seventeen, he was taught to kill people to solve problems.

As he told me these war stories, a memory surfaced—one I hadn't thought of in years. As a young child, I had found him in the middle of the night curled up in the bathtub, sobbing. Not knowing what to do, I peed and ran back to bed. I had never told anyone, but at that moment, it came back vividly.

My father's childhood and his time as a seventeen-year-old soldier fighting for survival and learning to kill at such a formative age had never occurred to me. Over time, my heart softened toward him.

Now it was time for me to move to Omaha, and my father and I stood on his front lawn.

"I won't be alive when you come back," he said.

I couldn't help but feel sorry for him. The man who neglected and abused me, who had inflicted so much pain on so many—was now just a lonely old man, assuming that his words would, or even could, matter to me or anyone after the choices he'd made.

"You're too mean to die that soon," I said, laughing. "Just write me."

He tightened his lips. "I hate lawyers. They're all crooked, you know." That was his way. If manipulation didn't work, he'd turn to anger. But it didn't matter anymore. I'd given enough.

I got into my red Mustang and drove away. I could see him in the rearview mirror, watching me.

Chapter 37

All Star

We made the ten-hour drive to Omaha with Quincy's parents in August of 1999. It felt as though they were sending us off to college. They stayed with us for a week and helped us settle into our rent house. It didn't have a fence, so Quincy and his father built one with chicken wire, while his mother and I cleaned the entire place from top to bottom. It was an old wooden house with an eerie basement that I refused to go into alone. A week later, orientation day arrived.

That morning, it was sunny and, in the mid-seventies. I had a coke and yogurt with granola for breakfast and then headed out the door to where Quincy was waiting for me in the car. He drove us to the law school and when we arrived, parking was limited.

Unlike in Texas, Omahans park on the street everywhere, which made parallel parking a necessity—a skill I hadn't quite mastered back home. What was even more interesting, Omaha was all rolling hills, similar to San Francisco, which was an added challenge to parking. Quincy found a spot, and we rushed inside.

One hundred and fifty eager law students gathered for orientation and were waiting for the dean to join us in the auditorium. I had two minutes to spare, allowing me time to calm my nerves and people watch. The students' clothing choices surprised me. Some were dressed in sharp three-piece suits as if they were going to court, while others looked as if they had just rolled out of bed. I'd opted for something in between—Calvin Klein jeans, a cute tee, and sandals, which was a mistake because my feet felt like blocks of ice. I made a mental note to wear a sweater the next day.

The song "All Star" by Smash Mouth blared through the speakers, and the students' reactions were as diverse as their outfits, with some bobbing their heads and singing, while others sat stoic. After thirty seconds, the song faded out, and the dean's speech began—far different from what I had expected. He emphasized the importance of approaching law school with dedication, but also reminded us to have fun along the way to prevent burnout. He concluded his speech with, "Remember this for the next three years. After graduation, A students will work for the B students, and the C students will run Fortune-five-hundred companies and the world." I'd never heard that before, but if he was right, I'd be running the world someday. I had anticipated a speech designed to strike fear into us—a calculated attempt to drive us to succeed in law school.

As I drove us home, I couldn't help but think that, since we'd dodged the infamous speech, maybe we'd also be spared the dreaded Socratic method. Time would tell.

While preparing for law school, I had already learned that the Socratic method was a relentless style of questioning, one in which professors put the student on the spot, often revealing gaps in their knowledge or logic. Instead of guiding them to answers, the method could feel like an intellectual interrogation, forcing students to defend their ideas under intense scrutiny. I worried about whether I could succeed under that kind of pressure. Some claimed it sharpened critical thinking, but for others, it created anxiety and a fear of failure—pushing some to the edge, sometimes even to death. I reassured myself by remembering how I had worked a full-time job while going to college at night, pulling fifteen-hour days—for seven years—and I had been practicing my speed reading techniques for a year. Whatever the professors threw at me, I was ready.

The next morning, on the first day of class, seventy-five students sat quietly waiting for class to begin—all wondering who would be called on first. My hands were trembling in my lap. I squeezed them together every few seconds for comfort, as I'd learned in counseling.

"Tina, if I want to sell you my watch, how do we create a contract?" he said, the sound of his voice echoing in the quiet room as he pulled up his sleeve to show me his gold watch. My body tingled and my heart raced. My words came out jumbled, but I thought I answered correctly. The three additional questions he asked made it clear I had not. The exercise was humbling. Despite the professor's encouragement with each additional question, I began to doubt if I had what it took to finish law school.

The next day, after a light lunch that did little to calm my butterflies, I walked into a stuffy classroom, with Quincy trailing behind me. The amphitheater-style setup of tiered rows of white desks rose from the floor. A slender grey-headed professor in khaki pants and a blue polo shirt stood at the bottom, framed by a large whiteboard. He began pacing as the students settled in, and you could cut the tension in the air with a knife.

"Look to your left. Now look to your right—one of you won't be here by the end of the year," the professor said. To my left sat a girl, some kind of genius from what I'd heard, and, to my right, sat Quincy. *I'm in trouble*, I thought.

FORTUNATELY, it turned out that only a few professors used the Socratic method, and even then it was a toned-down version. Creighton struck a good balance, creating an environment that felt more like a family instead of a traditional school. Most professors had open-door policies, welcoming students to discuss the law, engage in casual conversation, or even share personal problems— offering advice when asked.

Law school proved to be exactly what I needed. I was finally moving forward in my life. Then, just a few weeks into my studies, I got a call from Nan, my father's wife.

"Your father has stopped drinking," she said, so joyfully I could practically see her smile. "He's turning his life around." Nan was not a half-glass-full kind of lady, and I wasn't sure how to take her response. But what I did know was that, for a lifelong alcoholic, quitting cold turkey was suicide.

A month later, Nan called again to tell me they had hospitalized my father. Doctors didn't give him long to live, and she told me I should come home soon if I wanted to say goodbye. Several instructors warned me that missing one week of law school was equivalent to missing a month of undergraduate. One of them even said I would fail if I went home, but I was willing to take the risk, hoping my father would offer a deathbed confession about what really happened to my mother on the day she was shot.

"WHY ARE YOU HERE?" my father asked when I entered his hospital room. He was lying in bed, his head propped up on pillows, a single empty chair beside him. An adjustable table, which held a clear plastic cup and straw, and a small pitcher next to it, was within his reach. "You should be in school," he continued. "There's nothing you can do here; you wasted your time coming." He sounded annoyed with me, and even though it had only been a few minutes, I'd already had enough of him.

I walked to the waiting room, where Ivy, Aunt Colette, and Nan were talking.

After sitting down, I asked them to fill me in on what had happened. Nan explained that my father had gangrene in his leg, and they wanted to amputate. The doctor said that if they didn't take his leg, he would die—he had refused the operation, and nobody could convince him otherwise. He'd put a gun to his head a couple of months prior and it had misfired, barely grazing his ear. I was convinced he wanted to die, and he was right about one thing —there was nothing I could do. What I really needed was a meal and a good night's sleep to come up with a plan to get him to talk.

OVER THE NEXT TWO DAYS, several family members came to say their goodbyes. As they left his room, tears filled their eyes as my relatives shared with me that my father had made amends for all of his wrongdoings. They each talked of the peace and relief they felt after their visit. I looked forward to having a similar conversation with him, but more than anything, I wanted to know what happened the day my mother was shot.

At the end of the fourth day, with an increase in his morphine dosage, my father was beginning to fade. We were alone in his room; it was cold and sterile. I sat in the chair next to his bed, staring up at the television where it hung near the ceiling.

"Can you do me a favor?" He suddenly asked.

I stood, expecting to hand him his water cup or adjust his pillow. "I know you've talked with my first wife's daughters," he said. "Can you tell them I'm sorry? But also tell them it was their mother's fault I didn't get to see them."

"Well, if I can find them, sure."

I sat back down. *Any minute now*, I thought. *It'll be my turn. He's going to make an apology and tell me what really happened that dreadful day.*

"Hey, can you see that plum tree?" he asked instead, his voice low. He pointed to the corner of the room.

"No, I can't see it."

"Oh, it looks like the tree I sat under when I was a boy. I must be hallucinating." He laughed. I'd been waiting for several days for my goodbye speech, and I couldn't wait any longer. I jumped up from the chair and said, "Daddy, is there anything you wanted to say to me before I have to leave?"

"What would I say to you?"

"You've apologized to every person in the world but me."

He sneered. "You should be grateful for how I treated you. I made you who you are today."

I sat back down, and he drifted off to sleep. I stayed with him for a while, watching as his breathing slowed. In the wee hours of the morning, I drove back to Omaha. Two days later, my father died.

Chapter 38

Sink or Swim

I spent the next ten weeks catching up on schoolwork. By the time finals came around, I was sick from stress and lack of sleep. After taking my last exam, I was sure I'd failed my first semester of law school—and although I didn't fail, I came damn close. I slipped into a debilitating depression. I began sleeping twelve hours a day and barely getting up to eat or interact with Quincy.

I had fought against taking antidepressants for five years. For me, taking medication felt like defeat. But my law school mentor and counselor both insisted I should take them. If I didn't do something, I would not finish, like my professors had warned me. I began taking a selective serotonin reuptake inhibitor a week before the spring semester of my first year of law school. Within five days, I felt numb, but like a new person at the same time. I charged into the next semester, feeling like I could conquer the world. But as luck would have it, things were never that easy. I had worked on my codependency issues for several years, but I had continued to struggle with saying "no" when people asked for my help.

THE WEEKEND before my second semester of my first year, I received a call from Brandy's daughter, JJ. She was an infant the last time I had seen her and taken care of her for two weeks when I was eleven years old. I had attempted to contact her over the years, but her Grandma wouldn't allow it—since I was Brandy's sister—I had to be no good. I'd received a couple of letters with pictures when she was maybe seven years old, but nothing else for ten years, even though I had written to her several times. I'd been waiting for this day.

"Aunt Tina," she said when I picked up, "this is JJ. I can't live here anymore with my Nana and Papa, and they said I could come to Texas and live with you if you'd let me." My mouth flew wide open, and my hand shook as I looked around for Quincy—I'd been waiting to meet her for so long. I stuttered a little and asked to speak to her grandmother.

"Tina, I can't take this anymore," her grandmother told me. "JJ thinks you and her Texas family are better than us—she's failing school, uncontrollable, and I'm ready to let you have her—will you take her?" She sounded frantic.

Without hesitation, I said, "Yes, but I live in Omaha and need to confirm with my husband that he is okay with this arrangement."

A few days later, we were pseudo parents to a seventeen-year-old young lady who was in her senior year of high school and might not graduate because her grades were so low. JJ's high school was across the street from the law school, and every day, after school, she had to walk over to the law library and study with us until dinner time—we had set clear boundaries, and this was a non-negotiable.

After the first six weeks, she was making ones and twos, which were equivalent to As and Bs. I remember the look of shock on her face when she came to me and said, "I thought I was stupid all these years—but I just needed to do my homework?" I laughed and said, "Yep, it's a wonder what a little studying can do."

As we approached the end of the semester, JJ realized life would not be easier with us and she called her grandmother, telling her she was homesick. We wanted JJ to finish the semester before going back home, since she had been doing so well in school. Her grandmother was thrilled to hear the news that JJ was homesick and said, "I didn't think she'd last two weeks, but thank you for taking good care of her and making sure she will graduate." At the end of the semester, JJ went back home.

That summer, I took a couple of classes and worked at the Douglas County District Attorney's Office in the Domestic Violence Division. It was a nice break from the rigid schedule during the first year of law school. Quincy had joined the Army Reserve and was gone all summer. He returned in early August, a couple of weeks before our fall semester began. His return home was anticlimactic, and I felt a distance between us that hadn't been there before. I didn't have time to beg him to tell me what was bothering him anymore—I was drowning, and it was time for him to sink or swim.

Chapter 39

Graduation

My second year of law school started off strong, and I was determined to raise my grade point average—until I got sick in October. The on campus clinic diagnosed me with a cold that turned into bronchitis and then pneumonia. By November, I had developed asthma and slept ten hours a day. My professors all worked with me on attendance, but I feared I would not do well on my final exams yet again.

Two months later, I crawled out of bed and shivered all the way to the bathroom, wheezing the entire time—it must have been sixty-five degrees inside the house that morning. I brushed my teeth, threw on a hat, and slid down the icy roads to get out of my neighborhood. I was determined to make it to my pulmonologist appointment for my allergy testing results.

On the way, I prayed for answers—something to explain my mysterious illness. My FBI physical fitness test was only eight weeks away, and I needed this resolved now. As I walked through the parking lot to the front doors of the medical facility, the wind cut through my jeans, the snot dripping from my nose froze mid drip, and snow covered my hiking boots. As I stepped onto the elevator, the soft classical music reminded me of childhood car rides with my mother.

I barely had time to sit before the nurse called my name and led me to an exam room. Moments later, Dr. Sharma busted through the door, his voice bright with enthusiasm. "I have good news. We found your problem—you are severely allergic to cats and somewhat to dogs."

"How long do you think it will take me to get better? I have a physical fitness test in eight weeks with the FBI."

"Oh, Ms. Tina, I actually administer those tests for them, and I'm sorry to tell you that you won't be able to pass the pulmonary function test."

"Do you mean now, or never?"

"Do you really want to work for the FBI?" he asked.

I was sobbing. "Yes, more than anything," I said, looking down at my shoes.

"I can help you pass. Since you'll be a lawyer and not a field agent, it's not a big deal." The tone of his voice changed—It sounded more serious than a moment ago, and this awful feeling in my gut suddenly hit me. The same one I had sensed as a teenager.

"Is it legal?" I asked.

"I help many people like you pass the PFC test. Think about it, and I'll see you next week for your first allergy shot, and you can let me know if you want my help then."

Finals were only two weeks away, and after three rounds of antibiotics and a round of steroids, I was finally getting better. As I studied, my mind wandered: *What kind of help can Dr. Sharma provide? Would this be considered cheating?*

The weight of the decision was too much for me. My mind spun in circles. I remembered the night the two detectives laughed all the way out the door when I told them I wanted to be an FBI agent. No matter my choice regarding whatever it was Dr. Sharma was alluding to, regret would follow, and I only had a few days to decide.

I asked Quincy what he would do, and, without wavering, he said, "No one will know—it's doctor-patient privilege—and, like he said, you aren't going to be a field agent, so I don't see it being a big deal." I still felt uneasy about the whole thing. Two other friends, one in law school and one back home, both agreed with Quincy, but for different reasons. But the pit of my stomach had been aching every day since I had left Dr. Sharma's office, and that had to mean something.

I immediately noticed Dr. Sharma in the hallway when I stepped off the elevator. He paused, offering a warm smile. "Ms. Tina, how are you today? You're going to see the nurse for your first allergy shot, but have you made a decision about what we discussed last week?"

My stomach turned. For a second, I thought I might throw up right there on his shoes. "I'm not going to need your help," I said, forcing the words out. "But thank you for the offer."

His eyebrows shot up in surprise. "Really? You don't want my help?"

I swallowed hard. "No, of course I do. But it feels like cheating, and I can't do it," I admitted as a tear slipped down each cheek.

Dr. Sharma studied me for a moment, then nodded. "Ms. Tina, no one has ever said no before. I've often wondered if I'd ever meet someone who would." His voice softened. "You're going to have a good life, no matter what you do. Becoming a lawyer isn't easy, and I'm sure your parents are very proud of you."

I felt lighter walking out of the building, as though a weight had been lifted. But by the time I reached my car, the tears were flowing hard. I could barely see for the fifteen minute drive home, but I made it. I climbed the stairs to my room, collapsed onto my bed and cried myself to sleep.

I took my finals the following week and pushed the FBI out of my mind for good. Spring classes were around the corner, and it was time to refocus.

IN JANUARY OF 2001, Quincy and I started our second semester of our second year of law school. I hoped this semester would be different, and I'd have more time to focus, study more, and finally make better grades. I had some elective classes on my schedule, Bankruptcy and Taxation, they were my favorites.

But just as things started to settle, my phone rang. It was my cousin Tara.

"Listen here—you need to get your ass back to Texas and pick up your sister and take her back with you to Omaha. She's been hospitalized twice, and we're sick of taking care of her."

Ivy was only in her mid-thirties, and more than likely her health issues were drug related. But the cousins had reached their limit, and now the responsibility was being tossed into my lap.

I placed the receiver back on the cradle, and turned to Quincy, who'd been listening to my end of the conversation, and I said, "She's not my problem, right? I'm barely surviving as it is." We had already helped Ivy move from El Paso back to Dallas a few years ago. I began to sweat, and my pulse quickened. The thought of moving her again felt overwhelming.

Quincy's response came as a surprise. "She did so well when she lived with us before. Maybe we should help her." He paused and then added, "I feel sorry for her, Tina—I feel like I understand her in a way that you don't. You should go get her—she's your sister." He was right. I didn't understand, but I didn't have the time or energy to fight either—and I caved.

I booked a flight to Dallas and I packed Ivy's belongings into a small U-Haul truck and moved her—and her dog and cat—in with us. By the end of my second year of law school, her relocation to Omaha had been relatively easy and her presence around the house had been a pleasant change of pace for us.

OUR THIRD YEAR of law school finally arrived, and I could see the light at the end of the tunnel. Ivy had been attending classes at the local community college to become a paralegal, and she was doing well. That semester flew by without any major hiccups and life was smooth sailing. I knew 2002 was going to be my year!

I was working at Creighton's legal clinic that semester. We helped low income clients, many who had been victims of domestic violence. It was emotionally tough on me at times. I'd try not to tear up listening to clients' stories about how they and sometimes their children had been abused. But sometimes it was impossible, and I would share a little tidbit of my story—something that was appropriate and would give the client a glimmer of hope to keep fighting for themselves and their children, even though sometimes it seemed easier to go back to the abuser. My hope was that they could see that great things were ahead for them too, if they hung in there just a little bit longer.

I had my first divorce trial in March of 2002, two months before graduation. The legal clinic represented a woman who had been abused by her husband—she had three kids. I spent a week preparing for trial. Thoughts would creep in about my mother and what my sisters and I went through. But I'd push them down and press on.

The director of the legal clinic sat next to me at trial, but only to observe. I called all the shots. The husband didn't show up to court. So, of course we won.

The trial was painfully slow for everyone, even me, because I had overprepared. After we finished, I asked the judge for constructive criticism while I packed up all of my papers. He smiled and said, "You did a great job, but next time, speed up your questioning. Using an outline instead of typing out each question verbatim will help."

"Your Honor, rest assured I will never do that again." Everyone laughed as we walked out of the courtroom. Driving home, I couldn't help but think about how my life would have been different if my mother had been able to find a legal clinic to help her—maybe she'd even be alive right now. I cried tears of joy and tears of sadness that day, something I'd never done before. But as the weeks pressed on and graduation neared, my depression crept back in—and I couldn't, for the life of me, figure out why.

The first few days in May, I couldn't shake the sense of doom. Then I realized my mother's birthday was just days away. My body always seemed to remember, even when my mind tried to forget. Mother's Day would be next, and then the anniversary of her death —May seventeenth.

The Friday before Mother's Day, Ivy asked, "Do you know what day you are graduating on?"

"No, why?"

"It's the anniversary of Mama's death. I can't believe you didn't remember! Isn't that weird?"

I smiled and said, "Nope, that was God." Mason's mother, Judy, had told me that many times, and it had always stuck with me. It was affirmation that my mother was with me in my heart, and even though she couldn't be there in person, she was in spirit. I had an overwhelming sense of peace. I prayed "now I just have to pass the bar—I wonder how you're going to pull that one off?" I laughed to myself.

I had never been a big fan of celebrations. I was ready for graduation day to come and go so I could focus on preparing to take the bar exam in July. A few days later, we were back in Texas, and I immediately began studying my butt off.

Chapter 40

Endings

Quincy blurted out on New Year's Eve of 2002, "I want a divorce.". We'd just celebrated ten years of marriage. Arriving home from work around seven that evening, I noticed him sitting on the sofa with a gritty look on his face. Tension was in the air. I walked over to sit beside him, determined to keep my marriage together, and asked him to try counseling again. He argued that he'd made up his mind, but he ultimately relented, saying he was willing to give it another try. Although, his demeanor told a different story.

We'd been back in Texas for less than a year. After graduating law school in May of 2002, we had packed up and driven back to Texas. Ivy moved in with a friend, and we moved into our old house.

In June, while I studied for the bar exam, Quincy surfed the internet all day. While I was studying eight hours a day, five days a week, for eight weeks, he stared at a computer screen. If I wasn't hitting the books, I was delivering pizzas. The chances of me passing the bar on the first try were grim—not only had I attended an out-of-state law school, but I was still a terrible test taker. And we had arrived back in Texas too late to take the bar review prep course. I was on my own. Quincy, on the other hand, never seemed to fail at anything, so he didn't start studying until I finally put my foot down two weeks before the exam date.

Together, we sat for the bar exam at the end of July. A few weeks later, while waiting for the exam results, I started a new job at a downtown Dallas law firm.

In November, when the results arrived, not only did we learn I had failed, but that Quincy had failed too. Although I'd mentally prepared for failure to some extent, Quincy was devastated and became angry.

That weekend, as we discussed finances, Quincy suddenly stood up from the sofa and yelled, "You should have made me start studying sooner!" before storming out into the garage. I sat frozen on the couch where he left me. My two cats were staring at me, and I stared back, not knowing what to do. He'd never behaved that way. In our twelve years together, I'd only heard him raise his voice one other time, and it wasn't toward me.

During the first counseling session, Quincy agreed to continue working on the marriage, but only if he could move to his parents' house temporarily, staying there until after we took the February 2003 bar exam. He said it was so he could focus on studying, but deep down, I felt as though he had already made up his mind and was waiting for the right moment to call it quits.

The day after Quincy threatened divorce, I called a bar-review prep company to research the cost of taking their course. The young man on the other end of the phone asked me a few questions, and I answered.

"By the way, how many points were you off from passing?" he asked.

"Forty-five," I said.

After a moment of silence, he spoke again. "Listen, I've seen this a hundred times before, and I won't sugarcoat this. You'll never recover from this—you should find a new career."

I started to cry. "My life is falling apart, and becoming a lawyer is all I have. Are you telling me I can't take your course?"

"The cost is four thousand dollars," he said, "but you won't get the course for free if you fail again, since you scored so low the first time," he added, his sharp tone making me feel even worse.

I thought of my friend Megan that moved to California with her husband, Mark, who I had gone to law school with. He had taken a course called Celebration Law Review. The founder was a Christian, and they only focused on prepping students for the five hardest bar exams in the country. I ended up taking that bar prep course.

A FEW DAYS LATER, on my thirty-second birthday, Quincy moved out of the house for good, despite his promise to give our relationship a chance. While his mother would always fuss over my birthday, she was as absent as he was that day. Quincy's family was all that I had, and now it felt like that was all over. I'd not had a chance to reconnect with old friends in the short time we'd been back in Texas. I was alone and not sure I wanted to live anymore.

That evening, after feeding my dogs, Bear and Amanda, I stayed outside with them for a while. Bear, a black and white husky mix, was always eager to please. Amanda, a Doberman mix, stood ready to protect. They were a perfect balance of love and loyalty. Saying goodbye to them was the hardest part, but that was what I had to do—I didn't want to live anymore.

Slowly, I slid the glass door shut behind me, and watched them resting peacefully in their big doghouse. Tears streamed down my face. "They're going to be okay," I whispered, though I wasn't sure I believed it.

My mind played out the last twelve months. I thought about the year before—how Quincy had surprised me with a birthday trip to Las Vegas. He'd never done anything like that. What had changed? How did we get *here*? I wondered about the last six months. What had he really been doing? Was he looking for a job and studying for the bar exam like he said or had he already checked out of our life completely?

I walked into the spare room where Quincy had spent most of his days over the last six months. Being in that room gave me chills. Sitting in his swivel chair, I turned as I gazed at the bare walls and boxes stacked up everywhere. I spun back to the huge computer monitor on the desk. "Do I really want to know?" I asked myself. Maybe it was easier not to.

Instead of looking through the internet history, I clicked on Sheryl Crow's *Tuesday Night Music Club* while I sobbed and prayed. Why had I stayed with him? Why did he beg and plead with me to stay, just to leave me now? How was I going to pay seventy thousand dollars in debt by delivering pizza? I had graduated from law school at the bottom of my class. I would never pass the bar. *God, I thought you had a plan for me.*

When I stood, my legs were wobbly. Despite it being hard to see in the dark with swollen eyes, I made my way to my bedroom. The neighbor's lamppost illuminated the room just enough for me to find the nightstand where I kept my prescription medicines. I wondered as I rummaged for them if it would be enough to do the trick.

I found the small bottle of Xanax and shook it before popping the top off. I counted: one, two, three . . . There were ten in all.

I wasn't crying anymore as I brought the Xanax—my only option for relief—back to the spare room. I was on a mission. I placed the pills on the table, stared at them for a few minutes, and picked up a glass of stale water that had been sitting on the desk. With one gulp of water, I swallowed them all at once.

There weren't enough, I quickly realized. I needed something more to accomplish my goal.

I went to the kitchen to look for Quincy's allergy medicine, already feeling woozy and a little unsteady on my feet. All I found in the cabinet was a half-empty bottle of Benadryl.

With one hand gripping the counter and the other holding the bottle, I slid toward the refrigerator for something to wash them down. That's when I saw the bottle of vodka. I thought it odd to see it there, since we never had alcohol in the house. It was a sign; it had to be. Unscrewing the cap, I set it on the kitchen counter. The room spun, and I couldn't see clearly as I filled my palm with Benadryl. I knew I had only a little time before I passed out. I grabbed the bottle of booze, threw some pills in my mouth, and took a big swig. That was the last thing I remembered.

THE NEXT AFTERNOON, I felt myself being pushed into a sitting position. I was alone in my bed, yet it seemed like someone or something else was in the room—breathing life into me. I took a huge gulp of air, feeling like I'd just been saved from drowning.

I didn't know what was happening. My heart was pounding so hard I thought it might beat out of my chest, and I wanted to vomit. I crawled to the other side of the bed and reached for the phone.

When it was finally in my hand, I dialed my cousin. Although we hadn't spoken for years, he was the first person I thought of. He lived ten minutes away.

"Sam, it's Tina. I took some pills last night. I'm okay, just scared and dizzy. Can you come? But please don't tell anyone."

Chapter 41

Icy Roads

February came much too quickly. On test day, at five-thirty in the morning, Ivy yelled, "Wake up and get dressed! Let's go!" She insisted on driving me twenty-five miles on black icy roads, even though I'd already decided not to take the exam because I wasn't ready.

Two weeks before the big day, I had been sitting at my desk trying to study while consumed by the thoughts of my husband in a hotel with another woman—a random stranger had called to inform me that his wife was carrying on with my husband. He'd somehow gotten Quincy's number and was asking to speak with him. I let him know Quincy had moved out and I wasn't really certain if we were married anymore.

Whether it was true or not, how was I supposed to focus with something like that on my mind? I jumped to my feet and threw my books at the wall and screamed at God, "If you want me to pass, then you'll have to make it happen."

When the ice storm rolled in that weekend before the exam, I knew Dallas would shut down for several days. I was relieved because this would save me the humiliation of failing again. But on

Sunday evening, when I stood in the living room and told Ivy I wasn't going to take the bar exam Monday morning, she turned into someone I didn't recognize.

"Like hell you aren't!" she yelled. "I'll drive you myself. You can sleep while I'm driving."

Her reaction was out of character. Normally, she would say, "Fuck it, let's party." But there she was, encouraging me not to give up on my dream.

"I didn't watch you go through hell in law school to give up now. You're going," she said matter-of-factly, walking away to her bedroom.

"Whatever," I said. "It'll probably be canceled."

"Go to bed," Ivy said, slamming her door.

I turned off all the lights in the house and went to my bedroom. Bear and Amanda followed me and turned circles at the foot of my bed before settling in for the night. I lay in the dark staring at the ceiling and began praying: *I don't understand this life you've given me. Why is everything so hard? I feel like I've had my fair share of disappointments, and I want to do great things, but I'm tired and not sure how much more I can take. I'm going to need your strength to do this. I can't do it alone.*

That was the last thing I remember before falling asleep—Ivy was making such a racket in the kitchen that I decided to climb out of bed and get dressed. She was making coffee as I walked by her and out the front door. The frigid air blasted me in the face. It felt more like Nebraska than Texas. I ran to her old four-door, beat-up Toyota and crawled into the passenger seat, which was wonderfully warm and toasty. Ivy had evidently been warming the car for a while.

She drove twenty miles per hour, cautiously navigating the freeway that was a sheet of ice. Lying on my side, I stared out the window, just as I did as a kid. *Motley. La Prada. Buckner. St. Francis.* Two hours later, we arrived, and she nudged me on my back. "We're here," she said, handing me the coffee and fruit bar I hadn't touched. "I'll be here when you're done. Go, and good luck."

I blinked, still confused. "Thanks," I said sheepishly, closing the car door. She leaned back in her seat as I walked away.

I dropped into the passenger seat at five o'clock after the first day of testing and I barely said two words all the way home. The next day was a repeat of the first. By the third day, I felt energized and motivated to finish. After twenty hours of testing, I handed my final booklet to the proctor. "You'll get your results on May fifth," he said. Suddenly, this feeling rushed over me when I realized that was Mama's birthday. That had to be a sign from God that I would pass. And now that it was, everything would work out. In the meantime, there were two long months of waiting for results and I had to get busy living.

QUINCY FILED for divorce the day after I finished taking the bar exam.

I found a group of wonderful ladies at church to help me through this new chapter of my life. Some were married, some were widowed, some had been abandoned, and others were dealing with their husband's infidelity.

After delivering my news, one lady quietly said, "Disappointments come with following God." My logical brain could not comprehend what she said. And then, one by one, the women shared their stories. One woman told of her only daughter being stillborn. Another being left by her husband of thirty years when she had cancer. Another who found out her husband had another family after twenty years of marriage. Yet, all of these women had unwavering faith in "God's plan" even though they did not know the plan as it unfolded. Their stories baffled me, but also helped me to find peace.

I moved forward in faith. That's when I did what I do best—I made a plan. The next day, I informed my boss that I hadn't passed and that I would wrap up all my cases in the following two weeks. I knew he couldn't keep me on, so I planned to spend the summer by the pool as I studied for the next bar exam at the end of July. I would collect unemployment for the first time in my life. And with fewer distractions and a newfound faith, there was a better chance of passing this time around.

Chapter 42

Overcoming

When I walked into my boss's office the Monday after getting the exam results, he was sitting behind his desk reading *The Wall Street Journal* with a steaming cup of coffee sitting on his desk. Our office was on the tenth floor, and I could see out of his big office window the hustle and bustle of people walking to their high rise offices in downtown Dallas.

"How's my old hometown doing? And how was *The Phantom of the Opera*?" he asked as he quickly peeked his head over the newspaper. He didn't know I had canceled my weekend trip to New York City—where I was supposed to be celebrating passing the bar exam.

I didn't respond right away. Instead, I sat across from him in one of the two brown leather wingback chairs. "I'm not sure if you checked, but I failed the bar again," I confessed, my gaze fixed on my black leather satchel in my lap. A complete silence, heavy with unspoken words and disappointment, hung in the air as I finally met his eyes. "I'd let myself go too, but can I wrap up my projects over the next two weeks before I leave?"

"Sure, that will be just fine and helpful," he said with a heavy sigh. When he lifted the newspaper, the rustling of the pages signaled our conversation was over.

As I walked past her cubicle, my legal assistant mouthed to me, "I'm so sorry," her expression conveying deep regret. I simply nodded my head in acknowledgement, proceeded to my desk, and immediately began working. I knew that my focus for the next two weeks had to be completing all of my projects to make my departure easier for my boss.

TWO WEEKS LATER, on the Friday that was supposed to be my last day of work, Megan called to tell me her husband had passed the California bar and to tell me about the latest gossip on bar exams. She'd forgotten it was going to be my last day of work. But my boss had asked me to work the following Monday to complete one last project.

Megan began talking as soon as I said hello. "Hey, did you hear what happened in Illinois? There was a grading mistake. It's a shitshow."

"Wait. Slow down," I said.

She took a deep breath and began again. "Did you hear what happened in Illinois?"

"No. You know I don't watch the news."

"They stopped the swearing-in ceremony for the new lawyers in Illinois, because they discovered a grading mistake. There was a new company grading the multiple-choice part of this exam."

I was trying to follow what she was saying. "It looks like every state is affected—some states took away bar licenses from people who thought they had passed. It's a real shit show."

"A mistake, as in one multiple-choice question, was graded wrong?"

"Yes."

"There's no way one question is worth seven points," I said, doubting this would change my situation. I knew she was trying to give me hope, but I didn't want to let myself give into another fantasy.

"Well, maybe your god can do something about this, Tina," she said sarcastically. Megan was an atheist, and we'd had spirited discussions about religion.

I laughed. "Well, he certainly can, but that doesn't mean He will."

"It makes no sense. I don't understand how you still have faith in a God that let you fail the bar twice and now your husband's left you, too. I gotta go, but I still think you should call on Monday to see what's happening in Texas."

All weekend, my logical brain continued to dismiss the *maybe-I-passed* thought, as a pipedream. Spending time on remote and unlikely possibilities was a waste of energy.

ON MONDAY MORNING, as I drove to the office for my last day of work, the nagging voice in my head telling me to call would not stop, so I made the call. The phone rang twice before a weary-sounding woman answered. "Texas Board of Law Examiners, Linda speaking."

"Hi, there. My name is Tina. I failed the February bar, and I learned last Friday that there might be a grading mistake," I said, awkwardly. "Is there any chance David is available?"

She put me on hold.

A few minutes later, David came on the line. "Tina, it's crazy around here. We just found out Friday about the grading mistake, can I call you later?"

"Listen, David, I failed by seven points, and I know there is no way one question is worth that much, but I just had to check because I was fired and today's my last day at work."

"Of course, but I don't know anything yet. I promise I'll call you back this afternoon with some answers."

When I got to the office, I told my legal assistant what had happened, and that I was waiting for David's call. She seemed to be as anxious as I was. When the phone rang, she would grab it on the first ring so the other secretary couldn't answer.

Even though I tried to focus on my project, I felt a jolt of adrenaline run through my body whenever the phone rang and I'd lose my train of thought. Finally, my legal assistant answered the call I'd been waiting for.

"Oh my god, Tina," she said. "It's Carolyn from the State Bar on the phone."

I sat there frozen, staring at her.

"You have to pick it up. Carolyn is waiting."

My hand shook as I picked up the receiver. She introduced herself.

"I have you on speakerphone, Tina. David is here with me. He wanted to be here when I told you that you passed the bar exam."

"I passed?" I asked, while putting my hand on my chest, thinking I must have heard her wrong and then turning around to look at my legal assistant, who had been eavesdropping, and was staring at me in disbelief. She looked as surprised as I felt.

"Yes, Tina, you passed," she said in a soft and gentle voice.

"But how is that possible?" I asked.

"Any time there's an appeal, the entire test is regraded. In your case, this was a grading mistake, which we treated like an appeal. So, not only did you get credit for the one multiple-choice question you answered correctly, you also received extra points on your essays when they were graded again."

"I'm speechless. I can't believe this is happening."

"Your surprise is understandable. There's never been a grading mistake since the establishment of the Texas Board of Law Examiners. You and five other lawyers in Texas made history today."

"Carolyn, one last question—did anyone lose their bar license in Texas? I had heard other states took away bar licenses."

"No, absolutely not—we didn't think that would be an honorable thing to do—we're Texans, and better than that."

MY BOSS RETURNED from court a short time later, and I met him by the front door, which was only a few steps from his office. I explained all that had transpired. "Wow, that's quite a story," he said, raising his eyebrows and nodding simultaneously. "Go home and celebrate and we'll get you sworn in tomorrow, counselor."

Walking to my car, I held back the tears I'd been holding back for hours. Once I drove out of the garage, I sobbed for a few minutes as I thought about my mother—her beautiful smile, captivating laugh, and faith in God.

As I drove home, I pulled out my grey flip-phone out of my purse, pulled up the antenna and started calling people. I reached my cousin Tara first. I sailed right into my speech. "You are not going to believe this."

"What is it, baby girl?" she asked, sounding wary.

"I passed! I passed!"

"Did you really?"

"Yes, I answered the one question correctly, and they graded my essays again and I got a few extra points."

"Jesus literally moved mountains to get you to pass the bar—this is a real-life miracle!"

"I know, but I've got to call Megan, now," I said with urgency.

I closed the flip-phone and opened it again, punched in Megan's number. I had it memorized since we talked often. She answered on the second ring. "Hey, Tina! Did you find out anything today?"

"Guess what my God did?" I exclaimed.

"Really? Oh, my goodness, I'm so happy for you—you deserve this more than anyone I know." She shouted to her husband, "Honey, Tina passed! She passed!"

As I pulled into my driveway, we hung up the phone. I stayed in my car and cried some more. Then I asked Him, *Lord, did I fail the bar and then pass it two weeks later so that Megan could witness a miracle? For everyone who knows me to witness a miracle?"*

I received no answers, of course. I often joked that God and I operated on a need-to-know basis—and evidently, I didn't need to know. But one thing was certain: I hadn't passed the bar exam on my own!

And that was when it hit me. Every trial, tribulation, and hardship had been for a reason. They had shaped me, prepared me and led me to this exact moment in time. And intuitively, I knew that more struggles would be forthcoming.

That somehow didn't matter anymore, at least not for now. I would enjoy my win while I could. I still had my hands on the steering wheel. I let out a big sigh, rested my head back on the seat, and closed my eyes. There I was, standing at the basin sink in the beauty shop. I could feel the lather between my fingers as I shampooed my mother's hair, taking care not to miss a spot as I worked from the top of her forehead to the nape of her neck.

She opened her eyes only for a brief moment, and said, "See, *mija*—I was right, and you are going to do more great things."

Epilogue

Over the years, I shared bits and pieces of my story with friends, and I must have heard the words "You should write a book" at least a hundred times. When I started jotting things down in 2009, publishing a memoir was the last thing on my mind. I simply wanted to document my experiences—like a lawyer stating the facts of a case—so I wrote a twenty-seven-thousand word essay to preserve my memories and my past. But then, roughly ten years ago, I had an overwhelming feeling to expand those pages and share my story with the world. The idea felt ridiculous at first, but if there is one thing I've learned, it's to trust those internal promptings!

The road to completing this book has been harder than I could have ever imagined. I have faced setback after setback and spent enough money to put a child through college. But making money was never my intention. I wanted to inspire others to persevere through disappointments and heartbreaks, pursue their dreams, or create new ones if necessary—and most of all—to never give up.

Unexpectedly, and sometimes startlingly so, details from my

childhood came flooding back that sent me down an investigation rabbit hole.

Five months before publication, I was reviewing the scene in the book where I had learned my father wouldn't be living with me and my mother anymore, and a strange thought came to me. I wondered why he knocked on the door that day, instead of using his key—it wasn't his style not to barge in, even if she had asked him not to. Looking back on that moment, it was as if an invisible barrier had kept him out of the house. And for the first time, I had the thought—did my mother filed a restraining order against my father?

When I began my search online for the divorce case, I found yet another surprise: there were two cases. My mother had filed for divorce when I was three, but it had been dismissed. I never knew that.

I found the case I was looking for and ordered it from the courthouse. Sure enough, my mother had signed an affidavit stating my father had a violent and ungovernable temper, was unpredictable, and had abused and harassed her, causing her serious bodily injury during the marriage. But when I reviewed the Final Decree of Divorce, I noticed something unsettling—my mother's signature on the last page looked completely different from the one on her affidavit.

THE REALIZATION that my mother had filed a restraining order and the fact that she didn't even sign the divorce papers—gave me pause. Did my father have connections that could have helped him get away with murder? Could he have had leverage over the cops if they helped him cover up shootings while he was working at Miller's Drive-In? Is that why it took my father forty-five minutes to call 911? These new details made me want answers all over again.

Unfortunately, I don't have the one-page incident report or the five pages from Parkland Hospital that I ordered back in 1991, because Detective Bryan kept my documents "to show his supervisors." I was nineteen—and naïve—and hadn't asked for a copy.

In late December of 2024, I filled out the public records request for my mother's shooting and received seven pages in total. I've added them to the end of this chapter, but the key points are as follows.

The report, dated May 4, 1981, stated, "Sargent White entered the house, bent down and asked [my mother] had she shot herself and she said she did." Next, at the end of the paragraph, it said, "Paramedic stated patient said, 'Why would anybody want to hurt me no I don't to because he's the father of my kids.'" Clearly, some words are jumbled or missing here—perhaps someone was in a hurry—or the tone of my mother's statement doesn't align with her shooting herself? The last sentence of the report reads, "CAPERS # . . . asked that this offense be assigned to him and patient was taken to PMH be DFD . . ."

The affidavit my father signed at the police station stated that my mother had called him several times the day before, saying she needed to talk to him, and that, on the morning of the shooting, she called again and he went over to her house. According to him, she made a pot of coffee and pleaded that they get back together, to which he said no. He also stated that he asked her why she shot herself and she said, *If I can't have you, I want to die.*

The supplemental forensic report, dated May fifth, stated the "latent prints lifted were not comparable"—meaning the fingerprints on the gun could not be matched. It also stated that the "patient was unconscious on arrival to PMH and taken to surgery and has not regained consciousness since then. The witness, ex-husband, submitted to hand washings and the result of which was negative. The offense will be an attempt suicide."

A subsequent report stated, "Patient has died reassigned to CAPERS." The final supplemental report, created on June third stated, "Offense changed to a suicide ruled by Medical Examiner's office."

But I saw my mother conscious, so the report claiming she never regained consciousness was incorrect. Is that why there were only five pages of records at Parkland Hospital that said absolutely nothing that happened during her thirteen days in the Intensive Care Unit?

I CAN'T HELP but wonder why God allowed me to learn all this information now. It was He who planted the initial thought that led me down that rabbit hole. But I suppose I don't need to know —after all, He and I are still on a need-to-know basis.

Or maybe the answer will come later. With my life, I never know what's waiting around the corner. For many years, because of the very defining events of my life, I struggled to see a place beyond that corner. But things have their way of working out, if we keep moving forward in faith.

TODAY, I have my own law firm in a small town outside of Dallas. My law practice has evolved over the years, but the majority of my cases have consisted of divorces and custody battles, many of which involved abuse and domestic violence. I've not remarried yet. I don't have children of my own, but I've helped raise several over the years.

As for Brandy, she showed up at my doorstep in December of 2012 with six months to live. I hadn't heard from her since September of 1998, the year I deferred going to law school so that she could parole out to my house. During the six months I cared for her, God redeemed our relationship and I was at peace when she went home to the Lord. But she never would tell me anything else about the day my mother was shot except "I was asleep in the back of Uncle Chester's store in the loft—that's all I know." It was the same story she had told for years.

Ivy and I have had a rocky relationship over the last two decades, but we are a work in progress.

THE LAST THING I want to leave you with is this: Believe in yourself. Help others. Accept help when you need it. And know that if you persevere, great things will come.

OID KER   TCB - 1832   DALLAS POLICE DEPARTMENT   SERVICE ███████
                    REPRODUCED-3 ███ INCIDENT REPORT   DATE REPORTED 05/04/81

DISPATCHED TO: 00███   █████████   AT 1151 AS SIG:19

BEAT: ███   WATCH: 2   ELEMENT: 0902

COMP. NAME: ██████████████████   R/S/A: ████████
HOME ADDR: ███████ H██████   BUSN.ADDR.
DALLAS   N/A

OFF.LOC:00███████████████   APT.   DATES OF OCCURRENCE
PREMISES:RESID   PROP.ATT.CODE:501   MON, MAY 04, 1981 1151
INV.ASSGN:

OFFENSE/INCIDENT:ATTEMPT SUICIDE   UCR CODE 1:39050

M/O:
 WITH GUNN

STATUS: O JCR DISP:R   SPECIAL REPORT: FOLLOW UP:1F   REVIEWED BY: ████

SR CODE:5 RELATED REPORTS: WEATHER COND:CLOUDY

INV.DIV.NOTIFIED: ████████████   CAPERS

REPT.OFF:██████████████ ███   OTHER OFF:█████████ B ████████

INJURED   PERSON   INFORMATION
VICTIM TAKEN TO:PMH   BY:DFD726
INJURIES: COND:UNDETERMINED

NARRATIVE

RP STATED THAT COMP AD CALLED HIM SEVEN TIMES YESTERDAY ASKING HIM TO
COME OVER AND THAT COMP CALLED HIM ABOUT 0700 THIS MORNING SAYING "PLEAS
E COME OVER I GOT TO TALK TO YOU PLEASE COME OVER". RP STATED THAT HE
ARRIVED AT COMPS HOME ABOUT 1045 THEY SAT AT THE KITCHEN TABLE AND
TALKED OVER COFFEE. COMP WAS TYING TO GET HIM TO COME BACK TO HIM.
RP TOLD COMP IT WAS IMPOSSIBLE THEN COMP SAID "I'LL BE RIGHT BACK".
RP STATED THAT HE HEARD A SHOT AND RAN TO SEE, HE SAW COMP AS SHE FELL
TO THE LIVING ROOM FLOOR,AS SHE FELL THE GUN FELL FROM HER HAND. RP
CALLED POLICE AND AMBULANCE. ELEMENT ████ OFFICER ████████ STATED THAT
WHEN HE ENTERED THE HOUSE HE BENT DOWN AND ASKED COMP HAD SHE SHOT
HERSELF AND SHE SAID SHE DID. PARAMEDIC ████ STATED THAT COMP SAID
"WHY WOULD ANYBODY WANT TO HURT ME NO I DON'T TO CAUSE HES THE FATHER
OF MY KIDS". CAPERS█ ████ ASKED THAT THIS OFFENSE BE ASSIGNED TO HIM
COMP WAS TAKEN TO PMH BE ████████

OID RE██████████ ████ ███████   SERVICE # ████████ M
ATTEMPT SUICIDE   DATE REPORTED 05/09/01

`     COMPLAINANT/WITNESS  INFORMATION  1`

CODE NAME	R/S/A	HOME ADDRESS	BUSINESS ADDRESS
RP ██████	████████ ████ ██████	████████ ██ ████	

SUSPECT ARRESTED: -   PATROL SUPPLEMENT ATTACHED: -

`** END OF REPORT **`

188645-m

AFFIDAVIT IN ANY FACT
AFFIDAVIT IN ANY FACT

THE STATE OF TEXAS
COUNTY OF DALLAS

BEFORE ME,

a Notary Public in and for said County, State of Texas, on this day personally appeared

, W/M,

Business

Who, after being by me duly sworn, on oath deposes and says: My wife and I have been divorced since February of 1981. She called me on 5-4-81 at 10:30 A.M. at work and asked me to come over. When I arrived, she made a pot of coffee. We started drinking coffee, and she asked me to go back with her. I told her no and she got up and went towards the living room. I heard one shot then come from the living room area. I ran to the room and saw her standing up, holding a gun to her belly. She dropped the gun and fell to the ground. I asked her why she shot herself, and she said, "If I can't have you, I want to die." I then called the operator to get an ambulance. My ex-wife has had my pistol, a .38 caliber pistol, for the last two weeks because she said someone had threatened her.xxxxxxxxxxxxxxxxxxxxxxxxxxxxxxxxx
xxxxxxxxxxxxxxxxxxxxxxxxxxxxxxxxxxxxxxxxxxxxxxxxxxxxxxxxxxxxxxxxxxxxxxxxxxxxxxxxxxxxxx
xxxxxxxxxxxxx

xxxxxxxxxxxxxxxxxxxxxxx xxxxxxxxxxxxxxxxxxxxxxxxxxxxxxxxxxxxxxxxxxxxxxxx

SUBSCRIBED AND SWORN TO BEFORE ME THIS 4th DAY OF _____ MAY, _____ A.D. 19 81

Notary Public, Dallas County, Texas

Form 64 — 101A
E46-123-0001

INVESTIGATIVE SUPPLEMENT REPORT
DALLAS POLICE DEPARTMENT

REPRODUCED-3

(1) COMPLAINANT (LAST NAME FIRST)				(2) LOCATION OF OFFENSE			(3) SERVICE NO
■		■	■	■			■

(5) OFFENSE AS REPORTED AND DATE			(6) DATE OF THIS REPORT	(7) PAGE		(8) CLASSIFICATION	(9) ARREST NO
Unexplained Shooting	5-4-81		5-4-81	1	1	39050	

	(10) YEAR	(11) MAKE	(12) STYLE	(13) MODEL	(14) LIC YR STATE NO	(15) VALID TAG NO	(16) VIN
RECOVERED STOLEN VEHICLE							

(17) LOCATION RECOVERED	(18) DATE REC	(19) BEAT REC	(20) OFFICER MAKING RECOVERY	(25) STATUS RECOMMENDATION
				☐ OPEN ☐ SUSPENDED ☐ CLOSED

(21) CONDITION OF VEH.	LIST ITEMS STRIPPED IN NARRATIVE	☐ CLEARED BY ARREST
☐ DAMAGED ☐ WRECKED ☐ BURNED ☐ STRIPPED ☐ UNK		☐ CLEARED BY EXCEPTIONAL ARREST ☐ CLEARED BY JUVENILE ARREST

(22) METHOD USED		(23) DESCRIBE LOC. OF RECOVERY	(24) DISPOSITION	☐ UNFOUNDED
☐ TOWED ☐ HOT WIRED	☐ KEY IN VEH ☐ OTHER ☐ UNK.		☐ AUTO ☐ RELEASED POUND TO OWNER	☐ CLASSIFICATION CHANGED

(26)   SHORT FORM SUPPLEMENT INFORMATION:

☐ CONTACTED COMPLAINANT NO ADDITIONAL INFORMATION	☐ CONTACTED WITNESS/S LISTED NO ADDITIONAL INFORMATION	☐ UNABLE TO CONTACT COMPLAINANT AND/OR WITNESS/S LISTED
DATE AND TIME	DATE AND TIME	DATE AND TIME

(27) NARRATIVE

The complainant was shot in the abdomen.

02-01-1 Ph. / Residen

Color photographs were taken of the residence.

A Smith & Wesson revolver, Serial 067658, model 036 was processed for latent prints.
Also the four cartridges and one cartridge case that were in the cylinder. The latent
prints lifted were not comparable.

2A-02-1 handwashing / ■

Handwashings were taken of ■ ■, white male ■.

31-02-1 Pistol/Scene

The handwashings, weapon and cartridges were submitted to the Institute of Forensic
Science on Tag 0366755 for analysis. Complainant's blouse received from ■

Determine if gun shot residue is present on handwashings.

Revolver – perform powder burns test and compare against missile off recovered from
Parkland Memorial Hospital.

Four cartridge cases – use in test firing

Blouse – use for powder burn test.

REQUESTED BY	Disp.	EL 434 FOR		(28) TOTAL PROPERTY VALUE REPORTED TO DATE	
REC'D BY	Stowe	ANSWERED BY		STOLEN	RECOVERED
TCR 12:00 PM TCD 12:02 PM TC6 12:55 PM TCC 2:00 PM					

(29) REPORTING OFFICER	I.D.	(30) SUPERVISOR APPROVING RANK I.D.	(31) SUSPECT DESCRIPTION ATTACHED
■	■	■ ■	☐ YES ☐ NO

(32) STATUS	(33) REVIEWER	(34) U.C.R. DISPOSITION
☐ OPEN ☐ SUSPENDED ☐ CLOSED	■	

STAFF REVIEW

Page ___ of ___

INVESTIGATIVE SUPPLEMENT REPORT
DALLAS POLICE DEPARTMENT

(1) COMPLAINANT (LAST NAME FIRST)	(2) LOCATION OF OFFENSE	(3) BEAT	(4) SERVICE NO
████████	████████		████████

(5) OFFENSE AS REPORTED AND DATE	(6) DATE OF THIS REPORT	(7) PAGE	(8) CLASSIFICATION	(9) ARREST NO
Att. Suicide 5-4-81	5-11-81	1-1	39250	

	(10) YEAR	(11) MAKE	(12) STYLE	(13) MODEL	(14) LIC YR STATE NO	(15) VALID TAG NO	(16) VIN

RECOVERED STOLEN VEHICLE

(17) LOCATION RECOVERED	(18) DATE REC	(19) BEAT REC	(20) OFFICER MAKING RECOVERY	(25) STATUS RECOMMENDATION
				☐ OPEN ☐ SUSPENDED ☒ CLOSED

(21) CONDITION OF VEH
☐ DAMAGED ☐ WRECKED ☐ BURNED ☐ STRIPPED ☐ UNK.

LIST ITEMS STRIPPED IN NARRATIVE

☐ CLEARED BY ARREST
☐ CLEARED BY EXCEPTIONAL ARREST
☐ CLEARED BY JUVENILE ARREST
☐ UNFOUNDED
☐ CLASSIFICATION CHANGED

(22) METHOD USED
☐ TOWED ☐ KEY IN VEH
☐ NOT WIRED ☐ OTHER
☐ UNK.

(23) DESCRIBE LOC OF RECOVERY

(24) DISPOSITION
☐ AUTO ☐ RELEASED
POUND TO OWNER

(26) SHORT FORM SUPPLEMENT INFORMATION:

☐ CONTACTED COMPLAINANT NO ADDITIONAL INFORMATION

☒ CONTACTED WITNESS/S LISTED NO ADDITIONAL INFORMATION
5-4-81 / 1:00 pm

☐ UNABLE TO CONTACT COMPLAINANT AND/OR WITNESS/S LISTED

DATE AND TIME   DATE AND TIME   DATE AND TIME

(27) NARRATIVE

THE COMPL. ON THIS OFFENSE WAS TAKEN TO PARK AFTER
SHE STATED TO THE RPT. OFF. THAT SHE HAD
SHOT HERSELF. THE COMPL. WAS UNCONSCIOUS ON
ARRIVAL AT PARK AND TAKEN TO SURGERY, AND
HAS NOT REGAINED CONSCIOUSNESS SINCE THEN.
THE OFF., ████████ W/M/ ████ CAME TO
CLAIMS AND GAVE ATTACHED AFFIDAVIT AND
SUBMITTED TO A HANDWASHING TEST, THE RESULTS
OF WHICH WERE NEGATIVE BY THE I.F.S.
LAB.
THIS OFFENSE WILL BE AN ATTEMPT SUICIDE
WITH NO FURTHER POLICE ACTION.

5 C

(28) TOTAL PROPERTY VALUE REPORTED TO DATE	
STOLEN	RECOVERED

(29) REPORTING OFFICER	I.D.	(30) SUPERVISOR APPROVING	RANK	I.D.	(31) SUSPECT DESCRIPTION ATTACHED
████		Sgt- ████			☐ YES ☐ NO

(32) STATUS
☐ OPEN ☐ SUSPENDED ☒ CLOSED

(33) DATE REVIEWED

STAFF REVIEW

(34) U.C.R. DISPOSITION
Closed

INVESTIGATIVE SUPPLEMENT REPORT
DALLAS POLICE DEPARTMENT

(1) COMPLAINANT (LAST NAME FIRST)	(2) LOCATION OF OFFENSE	(3) BEAT	(4) SERVICE NO.

(5) OFFENSE AS REPORTED AND DATE /	(6) DATE OF THIS REPORT	(7) PAGE	(8) CLASSIFICATION	(9) ARREST NO
A.H. Suicide 5-4-81	5-21-81	1 of 1	39050	

RECOVERED STOLEN VEHICLE

(10) YEAR	(11) MAKE	(12) STYLE	(13) MODEL	(14) LIC. YR STATE NO	(15) VALID TAG NO	(16) VIN

(17) LOCATION RECOVERED | (18) DATE REC | (19) BEAT REC | (20) OFFICER MAKING RECOVERY

(21) STATUS RECOMMENDATION
☐ OPEN ☐ SUSPENDED ☐ CLOSED

(21) CONDITION OF VEH
☐ DAMAGED ☐ WRECKED ☐ BURNED ☐ STRIPPED ☐ UNK

LIST ITEMS STRIPPED BY NARRATIVE

☐ CLEARED BY ARREST
☐ CLEARED BY EXCEPTIONAL ARREST
☐ CLEARED BY JUVENILE ARREST
☐ UNFOUNDED
☐ CLASSIFICATION CHANGED

(22) METHOD USED
☐ TOWED ☐ KEY IN VEH ☐ OTHER
☐ HOT WIRED ☐ UNK

(23) DESCRIBE LOC OF RECOVERY | (24) DISPOSITION
☐ AUTO ☐ RELEASED TO OWNER
POUND

(26) **SHORT FORM SUPPLEMENT INFORMATION:**

☐ CONTACTED COMPLAINANT NO ADDITIONAL INFORMATION
☐ CONTACTED WITNESS/S LISTED NO ADDITIONAL INFORMATION
☐ UNABLE TO CONTACT COMPLAINANT AND/OR WITNESS/S LISTED

DATE AND TIME | DATE AND TIME | DATE AND TIME

(27) NARRATIVE

This comp. has died. Reassign to CPERS.

QU 39050
38050

ASGN TO

(28) TOTAL PROPERTY VALUE REPORTED TO DATE

STOLEN | RECOVERED

(29) REPORTING OFFICER I.D. | (30) SUPERVISOR APPROVING RANK I.D. | (31) SUSPECT DESCRIPTION ATTACHED
☐ YES ☐ NO

(32) STATUS ☐ OPEN ☐ SUSPENDED ☐ CLOSED | (33) REVIEWED STATE REVIEW | (34) UCR DISPOSITION

Page ___ of ___

INVESTIGATIVE SUPPLEMENT REPORT
DALLAS POLICE DEPARTMENT

(1) COMPLAINANT (LAST NAME FIRST)	(2) LOCATION OF OFFENSE	(3) ▓▓▓	(4) SERVICE NO

(5) OFFENSE AS REPORTED AND DATE	(6) DATE OF THIS REPORT	(7) PAGE	(8) CLASSIFICATION	(9) ARREST NO
Att Suicide 5-4-81	6-3-81	1 1	39050	—

	(10) YEAR	(11) MAKE	(12) STYLE	(13) MODEL	(14) LIC YR STATE NO	(15) VALID TAG NO	(16) VIN

RECOVERED STOLEN VEHICLE

(17) LOCATION RECOVERED	(18) DATE REC	(19) BEAT REC	(20) OFFICER MAKING RECOVERY	(25) STATUS RECOMMENDATION
				☐ OPEN ☐ SUSPENDED ☒ CLOSED

(21) CONDITION OF VEH: ☐ DAMAGED ☐ WRECKED ☐ BURNED ☐ STRIPPED ☐ UNK

LIST ITEMS STRIPPED IN NARRATIVE

☐ CLEARED BY ARREST
☐ CLEARED BY EXCEPTIONAL ARREST
☐ CLEARED BY JUVENILE ARREST
☐ UNFOUNDED
☐ CLASSIFICATION CHANGED

(22) METHOD USED: ☐ TOWED ☐ HOT WIRED ☐ KEY IN VEH ☐ OTHER ☐ UNK

(23) DESCRIBE LOC OF RECOVERY

(24) DISPOSITION: ☐ AUTO POUND ☐ RELEASED TO OWNER

(26) **SHORT FORM SUPPLEMENT INFORMATION:**

☐ CONTACTED COMPLAINANT NO ADDITIONAL INFORMATION

DATE AND TIME

☐ CONTACTED WITNESS/S LISTED NO ADDITIONAL INFORMATION

DATE AND TIME

☐ UNABLE TO CONTACT COMPLAINANT AND/OR WITNESS/S LISTED

DATE AND TIME

(27) NARRATIVE:

2nd Supplement

The compl. was taken to Parkland after a self-inflicted GSW to the stomach, and died as a result of this wound on 5-12-81 at 2:30 am. The compl. was pronounced dead by Dr. ▓▓▓▓▓▓ who was notified by the M.E.'s office.

This offense was changed to a suicide and ruled by the M.E. office as a suicide.

5C

(28) TOTAL PROPERTY VALUE REPORTED TO DATE

STOLEN | RECOVERED

(29) REPORTING OFFICER

(30) SUPERVISOR APPROVING

(31) SUSPECT DESCRIPTION ATTACHED ☐ YES ☐ NO

(32) STATUS: ☐ OPEN ☐ SUSPENDED ☒ CLOSED

(33) REVIEWED

(34) UCR DISPOSITION Closed

Page 1 of 1

NO. _____

IN THE MATTER OF	§	IN THE DISTRICT COURT OF
THE MARRIAGE OF	§	DALLAS COUNTY, TEXAS
▉▉▉▉▉▉▉▉	§	_____ JUDICIAL DISTRICT
AND	§	
▉▉▉▉	§	
AND IN THE INTEREST OF	§	
▉▉▉▉▉▉▉▉	§	
▉▉▉▉▉▉▉, CHILDREN	§	

PETITIONER'S SUPPORTING
AFFIDAVIT FOR EXTRAORDINARY RELIEF

THE STATE OF TEXAS §

COUNTY OF DALLAS §

BEFORE ME, the undersigned authority, on this day personally appeared JO▉▉▉▉▉▉▉, who, being by me duly sworn, on oath stated:

"My name is JO▉▉▉, ▉▉▉▉▉. I am the Petitioner in the foregoing original petition for divorce."

"Respondent is capricious and irresponsible in the use of money and property and has expended funds and used property in a manner that is detrimental to Petitioner and the children. Petitioner reasonably fears Respondent will encumber, dispose of, waste, harm, conceal, or sell their property and dissipate the proceeds, depriving Petitioner of the property. Respondent is about to receive or has received approximately $5,000 as a judgment creditor which Petitioner fears will be concealed or disposed of by Respondent. Said money is needed by the parties to prevent repossession of or foreclosure upon certain items of community property."

"Respondent has a violent and ungovernable temper and is unpredictable. Respondent has abused and harassed Petitioner, and Petitioner has reason to be and is in fear of Respondent. Respondent has caused serious bodily injury to Petitioner during this marriage."

SIGNED THIS 27ᵗʰ day of _August_ , 1980.

Jo█████████ Affiant

SUBSCRIBED AND SWORN to before me this 27ᵗʰ day of _August_ , 1980.

Notary Public in and for Dallas County, Texas

My commission expires: _Aug 1981_

The Court finds that the Petitioner and Respondent have entered into an agreement for division of their estate and that the agreement is just and right.

IT IS DECREED that the agreement of Petitioner and Respondent for the division of their estate be and is approved and incorporated into this decree by reference as if it were recited herein verbatim.

IT IS DECREED that Petitioner and Respondent shall execute all instruments necessary to effect this decree and that Petitioner and Respondent have all appropriate and necessary writs, execution and process, as many and as often as is necessary to accomplish the execution and final disposition of this judgment.

All costs of court expended in this cause are adjudged against the party by whom incurred.

IT IS DECREED that all relief requested in this cause and not expressly granted herein be and is hereby denied.

SIGNED this 4th day of February, 19 81.

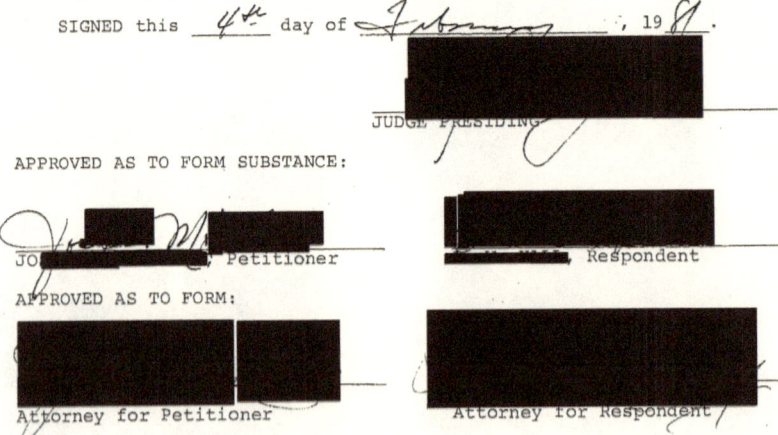

JUDGE PRESIDING

APPROVED AS TO FORM SUBSTANCE:

JO_____, Petitioner   Respondent

APPROVED AS TO FORM:

Attorney for Petitioner   Attorney for Respondent

www.ingramcontent.com/pod-product-compliance
Lightning Source LLC
Chambersburg PA
CBHW021221130626
46554CB00004B/1317